The Loeb-Leopold Case

Alvin V. Sellers

The Loeb-Leopold Case
The Loeb-Leopold Case
Alvin V. Sellers
HTR00158
Court Record
Yale Law Library
Brunswick, GA.: Classic Publishing Co. 1926

The Making of Modern Law collection of legal archives constitutes a genuine revolution in historical legal research because it opens up a wealth of rare and previously inaccessible sources in legal, constitutional, administrative, political, cultural, intellectual, and social history. This unique collection consists of three extensive archives that provide insight into more than 300 years of American and British history. These collections include:

Legal Treatises, 1800-1926: over 20,000 legal treatises provide a comprehensive collection in legal history, business and economics, politics and government.

Trials, 1600-1926: nearly 10,000 titles reveal the drama of famous, infamous, and obscure courtroom cases in America and the British Empire across three centuries.

Primary Sources, 1620-1926: includes reports, statutes and regulations in American history, including early state codes, municipal ordinances, constitutional conventions and compilations, and law dictionaries.

These archives provide a unique research tool for tracking the development of our modern legal system and how it has affected our culture, government, business – nearly every aspect of our everyday life. For the first time, these high-quality digital scans of original works are available via print-on-demand, making them readily accessible to libraries, students, independent scholars, and readers of all ages.

The BiblioLife Network

This project was made possible in part by the BiblioLife Network (BLN), a project aimed at addressing some of the huge challenges facing book preservationists around the world. The BLN includes libraries, library networks, archives, subject matter experts, online communities and library service providers. We believe every book ever published should be available as a high-quality print reproduction; printed on-demand anywhere in the world. This insures the ongoing accessibility of the content and helps generate sustainable revenue for the libraries and organizations that work to preserve these important materials.

The following book is in the "public domain" and represents an authentic reproduction of the text as printed by the original publisher. While we have attempted to accurately maintain the integrity of the original work, there are sometimes problems with the original work or the micro-film from which the books were digitized. This can result in minor errors in reproduction. Possible imperfections include missing and blurred pages, poor pictures, markings and other reproduction issues beyond our control. Because this work is culturally important, we have made it available as part of our commitment to protecting, preserving, and promoting the world's literature.

GUIDE TO FOLD-OUTS MAPS and OVERSIZED IMAGES

The book you are reading was digitized from microfilm captured over the past thirty to forty years. Years after the creation of the original microfilm, the book was converted to digital files and made available in an online database.

In an online database, page images do not need to conform to the size restrictions found in a printed book. When converting these images back into a printed bound book, the page sizes are standardized in ways that maintain the detail of the original. For large images, such as fold-out maps, the original page image is split into two or more pages

Guidelines used to determine how to split the page image follows:

• Some images are split vertically; large images require vertical and horizontal splits.
• For horizontal splits, the content is split left to right.
• For vertical splits, the content is split from top to bottom.
• For both vertical and horizontal splits, the image is processed from top left to bottom right.

THE LOEB-LEOPOLD CASE

PHILOSOPHY
From a Copley Print   by Puvis de Chavannes
Copyright by Curtis & Cameron Publishers Boston

PHILOSOPHY

THE LOEB–LEOPOLD CASE

WITH EXCERPTS FROM THE EVIDENCE OF
THE ALIENISTS AND INCLUDING THE
ARGUMENTS TO THE COURT BY
COUNSEL FOR THE PEOPLE
AND THE DEFENSE

BY
ALVIN V SELLERS

BRUNSWICK, GA.
CLASSIC PUBLISHING CO
1926

COPYRIGHT, 1926,
BY ALVIN V SELLERS

PRINTED IN THE U S A

CONTENTS

	PAGE
PHILOSOPHY . . . . *Frontispiece*	
THE LOEB–LEOPOLD CASE	11
Speech of Thomas Marshall	41
Speech of Joseph P. Savage	62
Speech of Walter Bachrach	90
Speech of Clarence Darrow	118
Speech of Benjamin C. Bachrach	214
Speech of Robert E. Crowe	233

THE LOEB-LEOPOLD CASE

The Loeb-Leopold Case

ON July 21, 1924, in the criminal court room of Cook County, Illinois, when the case of the People *vs.* Richard A Loeb and Nathan F Leopold, Jr, was called, Clarence Darrow, representing the defendants, arose, and addressing Chief Justice John R Caverley, presiding, said

> Your Honor, we have determined to withdraw our pleas of not guilty and enter pleas of guilty We dislike to throw this burden upon this court or any court We know its seriousness and its gravity And while we wish it could be otherwise we feel that it must be as we have chosen
>
> The statute provides, your Honor, that evidence may be offered in mitigation of the punishment, and we shall ask at such time as the court may direct that we be permitted to offer evidence as to the mental condition of these young men, to show the degree of responsibility they had, and also to offer evidence as to the youth of these defendants, and the fact of a plea of guilty as a further mitigation of the penalty in this case With that we throw ourselves upon the mercy of this court and this court alone

Young Loeb and Leopold had — just two months before — kidnaped and killed still younger Robert Franks All were sons of wealthy parents, and all residents of Chicago, where the crime was committed The slayers were college graduates.

The Loeb-Leopold Case

After the boy was murdered and his body hid in a culvert, Leopold telephoned to the home of Jacob Franks, father of Robert. To the mother, who answered the call, Leopold said· " This is George Johnson, your son has been kidnaped, don't worry, details later."

Early next morning the following letter was received at the Franks home, addressed to Jacob Franks

DEAR SIR

As you no doubt know by this time your son has been kidnaped. Allow us to assure you that he is at present well and safe. You need not fear any physical harm for him providing you live up carefully to the following instructions and such others as you will receive by future communications. Should you, however, disobey any of our instructions, even slightly, his death will be the penalty

1. For obvious reasons make absolutely no attempt to communicate with either the police authorities or any private agency. Should you already have communicated with the police, allow them to continue their investigations, but do not mention this letter

2. Secure before noon today $10,000. This money must be composed entirely of old bills of the following denominations $2,000 in $20 bills, $8,000 in $50 bills. The money must be old. Any attempt to include new or marked bills will render the entire venture futile. The money should be placed in a large cigar box or, if such is impossible, in a heavy cardboard box securely closed and wrapped in white paper. The wrapping paper should be sealed and all openings with sealing wax

3. Have the money thus prepared as directed above and remain home after one o clock P M. See that the telephone is not in use. You will receive a future communication instructing you as to your future course. As a final word of

warning, this is a strictly commercial proposition, and we are prepared to put our threats into execution should we have reasonable ground to believe that you have committed an infraction of the above instructions However should you carefully follow out our instructions to the letter, we can assure you that your son will be safely returned to you within six hours of our receipt of the money

Yours truly,
GEORGE JOHNSON

A few hours later the father was called by telephone and told to go to a designated drug store with the money, where he would again be called and given further instructions

He did not go, for, in the meantime, the dead body of his boy had been found in the culvert It developed that he was to have been directed to go immediately from the drug store to the Illinois Central Station and get aboard a certain train and in the telegraph blank rack of a certain Pullman car he would find a letter giving directions to be obeyed

This letter was in a plain envelope, addressed to "Mr Jacob Franks" Written on the envelope were these words. "Should anyone else find this note, please leave it alone, the letter is very important." The letter read as follows.

DEAR SIR

Proceed immediately to the back platform of the train, watch the east side of the track, have your package ready, look for the first LARGE red brick factory situated immediately adjoining the tracks on the east On top of this factory is a large black water tower with the word CHAM-

PION written on it. Wait until you have completely passed the south end of the factory, count five very rapidly and then immediately throw the package as far east as you can.
Remember, this is the only chance to recover your son.
Yours truly,
GEORGE JOHNSON

Near the culvert where the body was found was also found a pair of eyeglasses. From the records of the only concern in Chicago handling them it was learned that three prescriptions had been filled calling for that particular kind of glasses. One was for a prominent lawyer of the city, who was then out of town, another was for a lady, who had hers on, the other was for young Leopold, who, upon first being questioned, stated that his glasses were at his home. Upon being unable to find them there he said that he had not worn them for a long time and that he had taken many strolls through the section by the culvert and must have, on one of such occasions, dropped them from his pocket.

It was soon seen, however, that he and Loeb, who also had been taken into custody when it was learned he and Leopold were together on the day that Bobby Franks was kidnaped, were making false and contradictory statements. They continued to be questioned and proofs of their falsehoods shown them. It was not long before both confessed and gave in detail the story of this deed of death that stirred a world.

At the "trial" the defense asked life imprisonment while the State insisted on the maximum penalty of death

The State introduced the evidence of eighty-one witnesses — and rested. Every incriminating fact was proved, as being relevant on the question of "aggravation."

Then the defense began, with its evidence of "mitigation," followed by rebuttal evidence on the part of the State. The defense, though not disclaiming legal responsibility, urged, nevertheless, that the mental condition of the defendants was a mitigating circumstance. This the State vigorously controverted. Some excerpts from the evidence are given here. It would take volumes to include it all.

Dr. W. A. White was the first witness for the defense. He said in part:

> We can only understand this homicide by understanding the back and forth play of these two personalities as they are related to each other. Now, Dickie Loeb, with his feeling of inferiority, developed certain anti-social tendencies which are characterized to a certain extent to compensate him personally, but which are disintegrating and socially destructive, namely, his criminalistic tendencies. He develops these tendencies as being the head of a gang because, obviously, it is not half as satisfying to an individual to be a great man in secret. Dickie needed an audience. In his fantasies, the criminalistic gang was his audience. In reality, Babe Leopold was his audience. Babe is generally the slave in the situation. But he is a powerful slave, who makes Dickie king, so that in either position he occupies, as the king or slave, he gets the expression of both components of his make-up. All of Dickie's life has been in the direction of self-destruction. He has often considered suicide. He told me he had lived his life out, come to its logical conclusion.

Babe, on the other hand, has the definitely constructive capacities of an intellectual character

I do not believe that the Franks homicide can be explained without an understanding of this relation Babe would not have entered it alone, because he had no criminalistic tendencies, as Dickie did Dickie would never have gone as far as he did without Babe to give that final push

Dr White said that in his opinion neither Loeb nor Leopold was normal Of Loeb he further said:

He was the host of an infantile emotional make-up which was a long way from the possibility of functioning harmoniously with his developed intelligence He was going in the direction of a split personality, because of this inner, unresolved conflict It was that type of a personality, related as I have described to Babe, that came to this final issue on May 21, 1924

Q In your opinion was his mental condition on the 21st of May normal or otherwise?

A Decidedly otherwise He is still a little child talking to his Teddy bear

Extracts from the cross-examination of the witness by State's Attorney Crowe follow

Q Now, doctor, you said that young Loeb had no definite object in life, but he had decided to be a master criminal He made a pretty fair success of that until the glasses were dropped, didn't he?

A I don't know if we can talk of such a thing as being successful, he made a sad mess of his life, either whether he was caught or not

Q If the glasses had not been found, and the State's Attorney had not secured a confession, do you think these boys would have gone right along committing other crimes?

A I suspect they might have probably done so I do not see any reason why they would not

Q Now, which is responsible for the murder in this case, the emotional man or the intellectual man?

A Well, you cannot split a man up that way into two parts. When the man acts he acts as a whole.

Q Well, where does the crime originate, in the emotions or in the intellect?

A The emotions represent psychologically the instinctive drives of the individual. We would say action originated in the drive of the instincts. But that I don't believe would be a complete statement of the situation.

Q Will you explain how such an emotional infantile character as Loeb could appear so normal in all of his human contact?

A Unfortunately that is a very common experience with these people.

Q In your opinion did Richard Loeb, who appeared normal, yet had partaken in planning this murder to the minutest detail, have the power of choosing to carry out that plan or not? Answer yes or no.

A I can't answer it yes or no.

Mr Crowe Answer it any way you want to.

A Whether he could have avoided doing it or not is largely a metaphysical question. He did not avoid doing it, and so far as I can see inside of him, the powers that were at work within him at least impaired his capacity to choose very materially.

Q Are you able to tell from your examination of Richard Loeb whether or not on the 21st day of May, 1924, he knew the difference between right and wrong?

A He knew intellectually that murder was proscribed by the law.

Q Did he know it was morally wrong?

A He had no adequate feeling attitude toward its moral wrongfulness.

Q But did he have sufficient capacity to refrain from killing?

A I don't know.

Q Doctor, from your examination of Nathan Leopold, Jr,

The Loeb-Leopold Case

you are not able to tell whether he had the power of choice on May 21, 1924?

A I am not, and I do not believe any human being is

Q Do you know whether or not Nathan Leopold Jr, from your examination, knew the difference between right and wrong on that day?

A He knew it intellectually but he did not have the feeling attitude that was in conformity with such knowledge, in harmony with it

Q In your testimony you said Loeb was the master criminal of the two Is he the leader of the two in this crime?

A It is almost impossible to separate these two personalities The character of the act was the outgrowth much more of Dickie's way of thinking and feeling than of Babe's But the relationship that was maintained between them was largely maintained as the result of Babe's intellectual agility

Q Which one in your judgment has the stronger mind?

A I should say Babe had the most definite objectives He is building up something, if only defense On the other hand, Dickie's whole make-up impresses one as being more upon the other side of the equation, more of a tendency to disintegration, to follow along the lines of least resistance

Q You do not think that a young superintellectual like Leopold, who was studying law and preparing a defense, would try to mislead you?

A I wasn't very much frightened at any such possibility

Q Do you think that Nathan Leopold is capable of doing so?

A I don't know He hasn't in my opinion

Q Assume that he has fooled you and that the things that he has told you about himself which led you to the conclusion that you now have were all lies, then you would not have the same conclusion, would you?

A If things were all different from what they are, my conclusion in regard to them would be different from what it is

Dr William Healy testified next for the defense He said in part:

To my mind this crime is the result of diseased motivation — that is, in its planning and commission It was possible only because Leopold had these abnormal mental trends with the typical feelings and ideas of a paranoiac personality He needed these feelings and ideas supplemented by what Loeb could give him There is no reason why he should not commit the crime with his diseased notion Anything he wanted to do was right, even kidnaping and murder There was no place for sympathy and feeling to play any normal part In other words, he had an established pathological personality before he met Loeb but probably his activities would have taken other directions except for this chance association

Loeb's secret abnormal mental life swallowed up his ambition He is very friendly pleasant, well-mannered, a very charming boy, having many nice qualities on one side and yet on the other hand, having carried out for many years a dual personality, having been an extensive liar and a most unscrupulous individual, in a manner and to an extent that is quite beyond any in my experience He has shown a curious desire for sympathy in pathological ways, a desire to get along socially Contrasted with this is the fact that he is most remarkably unscrupulous untruthful, unfair, ungrateful, and disloyal in many social relationships, disloyal even to his comrade when he cheated him, and to his fraternity when he robbed them

He expresses, on the other hand, some loyalties to family life in certain ways and he has some well expressed and very decent ideas about girls

All of that, of course, shows a disparity and a contradiction that to my thinking is certainly abnormal The ability to carry on for many years this tremendously contradictory dual life is certainly pathological

Their association began at 15 years of age It is very clear that each came with peculiarities in his mental life, each arrived at these peculiarities by different routes, each supplemented the other's already constituted abnormal needs in

The Loeb-Leopold Case

a most unique way   In regard to the association, I think that I ought to say that the crime in its commission and in its background has features that are quite beyond anything in my experience   There seems to have been so little normal motivation, the matter was so long planned, so unfeelingly carried out, that it represents nothing that I have ever seen or heard of before   As judged by their conversation and by their correspondence, their compacts, their quarrels, their deeds, all tend to show a most strange and pathological relationship

Both Leopold and Loeb told me that drinking was considerable of a bond between them   The criminalistic activities of Loeb previously, according to his own account, began with his stealing in the neighborhood   In the matter of the association I have the boys story, told separately, about an incredibly absurd childish compact that bound them which bears out in Leopold's case particularly the thread and idea of his fantasy life   Loeb says the association gave him the opportunity of getting some one to carry out his criminalistic imaginings and conscious ideas   In the case of Leopold, the direct cause of his entering into criminalistic acts was this particularly childish compact

One sees Leopold exhibiting pretty definite signs of nervous instability, frequently shows a greatly exaggerated use of the muscles of the face, exhibiting many nervous gestures, ready flushings, and pallor   I also see signs in him of great nervous energy, and evidences of some pathology of the glands, of internal secretion, probably of the sympathetic nervous system   Concerning Leopold s mentality I find conclusive evidences, by a giving of a considerable number of mental tests, that he possesses very high intelligence

Leopold has developed logical methods of so-called neumonic devices, memory devices by which he can remember things in most remarkable fashion   You can make out a list of twenty words and he will read them over and then he can tell the order of those words, or if you tell him any one of the words he can tell which word came after it and which word came before it, and so on   His conversational powers are extremely good and he is, all through, very argumentative

Now, concerning his personality, one finds him extremely energetic, both physically and mentally. He does not want to stop after a half day of these arduous tests. It seems there is a great deal of what psychiatrists call pressure to mental activity, very little fatigue, and great desire to go on elaborating his thoughts. He showed himself to be self-centered and egotistic beyond any normal limit. He is extremely critical of other people and decidedly supercilious about his own mental attainments. Very stubborn in his opinions. He is right, the world is wrong. Leopold has extremely little sympathy or feelings or conceptions of gratitude except in some very narrow fields. There has been a tremendous subordination of many normal feelings and emotions to this excessively developed conception of himself as a superior individual, and he has reacted in a most abnormal way in regard to the whole crime. Leopold shows little disgust at jail surroundings. His main concern seems to be whether or not the reporters say the right thing about him.

There seems to be some steady impairment of his own judgment considering himself and his relationship to the realities of life, inasmuch as he has been so willing to throw away his remarkably fine chances in his environment for such petty awards in relation to a most heinous crime. An individual with normal judgment would have naturally developed his real superiority and not taken such extraordinary chances of ending his career.

He says that there is one thing that he is afraid that he has not ' gotten across to us scientists,' and that is, that the most important thing, much more important even than preserving his life is the preservation of his dignity.

Dr Healy here referred to Leopold's fantasy of the " king and the slave." He told how Leopold had identified himself with his " king " Loeb, and the physician produced a note Leopold had given him in court while Dr White was telling of this identification. The note said, "See poem I quoted you," and added

> *Let me dream once that dear delusion*
> *That I am you, O heart's desire*

Following is the poem which Dr. Healy said Leopold had previously quoted and with a good deal of apparent feeling

> *Long past the pulse and pain of passion,*
>   *Long left the limit of all love;*
> *I crave some nearer, fuller fashion,*
>   *Some unknown way, beyond, above,*
> *Some infinitely inner fusion,*
>   *As wave with water, flame with fire;*
> *Let me dream once that dear delusion*
>   *That I am you, O heart's desire.*

Q. Who is the poet that wrote that?
A. Lawrence Hope he tells me. In his fantasy there was a ready change about of himself with Loeb.

It appears to me to reflect a profound disorder of judgment, this contradictory existence of impulses and ideas which were living side by side. It indicates a spontaneously abnormal rift of tremendous contradiction between his intellectual precocity and his judgment and his emotional condition. There was no normal and consistent personality developed.

Leopold very early thought of himself as possibly a completely intelligent individual who might experiment with ideas of right and wrong and conscience and God.

Leopold's feverish mental activities have been made all the more possible because he has not, as he himself indicates, wasted any time on emotion.

Leopold expatiates nowadays on his own coldness as being desirable. He is now an intellectual who can keenly observe things. He can enjoy what he sees in jail, his own notes of the trial. He tells us that he has had considerable interest in observing himself as a murderer.

The Loeb-Leopold Case

Dr Bernard Glueck next testified in behalf of the defense

I took up the Franks crime with Loeb and asked him to tell me about it He recited to me in a most matter of fact way all of the grewsome details I was amazed at the absolute absence of any signs of normal feeling He showed no remorse, no regret no compassion and it became very evident to me that there was a profound disparity between the things that he was talking and thinking about, and the things that he claimed he had carried out The whole thing became incomprehensible to me, except on the basis of a disordered personality He told me how his little brother passed in review before him as a possible victim yet he showed the same lack of adequate emotional response His lack of emotion struck him as unusual when he sat listening to the testimony of Mrs Franks He came to explain it to himself as having nothing within him that might call forth a response to the situation

Mr Benjamin Bachrach Did Loeb say who it was that struck the blow on the head of Robert Franks with the chisel?

Dr Glueck He told me all the details of the crime, including the fact that he struck the blow

In response to further questions Dr Glueck said

My impression is very definite that Loeb is suffering from a disordered personality, that the nature of this disorder is primarily in a profound pathological discord between his intellectual and emotional life We might designate it as a split personality This boy, while capable of orienting himself intellectually, is quite incapable of endowing these surroundings with an adequate emotion

Speaking of Leopold the witness said

This boy has come to develop a definitely abnormal conception of himself, of his ego I am perfectly ready to place that conception of his ego within the category of what we know as paranoid. When I asked him whether he would object to having me detail some of the intimate things with respect to his instinctive life in a court room he said that he would rather hang than have me do so. He told me that people will still have a chance to consider him as possessing royal proclivities although these were directed into destructive channels. He told me if he went to the gallows that he would like to hold forth to show the world that he has been consistent to the very end.

Then followed the story of Leopold's early life, of his fantasy life, including the " king-slave " fantasy. Dr Glueck continued

He told me of his attitude toward Loeb, and of how completely he had put himself in the rôle of slave in connection with him. He said, " I can illustrate it to you by saying that I felt myself less than the dust beneath his feet," quoting from one of the poems of Lawrence Hope. He told me of his abject devotion to Loeb, saying that he was jealous of the food and drink that Loeb took, because he could not come as close to him as did the food and drink.

Nathan F Leopold, in my estimation, is a definitely paranoid personality, perhaps developing a definite paranoid psychosis. I have not seen a definite psychosis of this sort in as young a person as he is.

Q Doctor, from your experience, state whether or not it is ordinary to find in such persons a high degree of intelligence existing at the same time as the abnormality

A I should say that it is quite characteristic of paranoid individuals

Referring to the cross-examination of Dr Glueck the Chicago *Tribune* said

Mr Crowe, on cross-examination, sought to make Dr Glueck admit that Leopold and Loeb, in spite of their families' wealth, had kidnapped and murdered the son of the millionaire Jacob Franks, for a perfectly understandable motive — to get the $10,000 ransom

That the doctor in a quiet, steadfast way, refused to admit

Then, still seeking to travel that road that leads to the normalcy of the defendants, Mr Crowe insisted that Nathan and Richard, for all their heaped up advantages of heredity and environment simply were the black sheep of their respective families

Dr Glueck again refused to agree "I do not know the meaning of the term 'black sheep' in general," he declared "Furthermore, I've known many black sheep who were insane'

"Well," the prosecutor was persistent, "but what of the other black sheep you've known, the ones who weren't insane?"

Equally persistent was the doctor, as he smiled and replied "But they had psychological factors which might explain what they did"

Mr Crowe, unconvinced that the majority of such "black sheep" might be paranoiacs, pointed his irony as he clipped out "Now what about Benedict Arnold? He enjoyed the confidence and esteem of his fellow citizens, then he threw it away for position and money Was he a paranoiac?"

"I don't know" And Dr Glueck likewise pointed his irony

So the prosecutor took another example, as he shouted, "What about Judas Iscariot?"

The doctor from New York hadn't quite made up his mind whether to be annoyed or amused, when Judge Caverly, with genial neutrality in his tones, ventured the authoritative suggestion "I don't believe you ever examined him did you?"

Then Dr Glueck made up his mind He decided to be amused, not annoyed, as he answered "No, I don't believe I have"

And the last clash

Mr Crowe You say these defendants have told you everything about themselves Why didn't they tell me everything when they confessed the crime to me in the State's Attorney's office?

The Loeb-Leopold Case

Dr Glueck Because you are a prosecuting attorney, and I am a physician

That answer seemed satisfactory to everybody

Dr. H S Hulbert, who, together with Dr Karl M Bowman, had, at the request of the defense, made extensive observations of both defendants, was the next witness The combined report of these two experts was admitted in evidence and covered several thousand typewritten pages It included physical, neurological, educational, social and mental studies, and, in a novel way, it included researches in the physical chemistry and in the endocrine or glandular constitution of the defendants It appeared to these physicians that there was a causal relation between the biological make-up of the two defendants and their mental state. The main contributions to this crime were the disordered inner mental lives of Loeb and Leopold Loeb was a quiet chap with many friends but his life motive, which he had not disclosed, was the compelling desire to carry into realities the countless delusional phantasies of how he could supersede the hero of his childish excursion in literature, "The Master Criminal" In these pathological reveries he always had one accomplice When he reached the praecox age he sought an accomplice and found one in Leopold

Leopold, they said, had his life pattern stamped in early childhood by two governesses, one having introduced him to life in such a way that normal relationships would never be appealing nor satisfactory, and the other accidently inculcated upon his impressionable mind that he was superior to all he knew, but if he ever found someone superior to himself he should become the object, dutiful and unquestioning slave, of his "King" (cf "The St Christopher Legend") These ideas of superiority to criticism and to the ordinary code of social ethics and the ideas of being the perfect slave grew distortedly until he became delusional and irresistible He found in his neighbor, Loeb, an adequate sweetheart and what he regarded as a mind superior to his own to which he entered slavish bondage

Referring to Richard Loeb Dr Hulbert testified

My opinion is that the man is not normal physically or mentally, and there is a close relation between his physical abnormalities, largely of the endocrine system, and his mental condition Intellectually he far excels the average boy of his age But his emotional reactions are those — I estimate because I cannot measure — of a boy of about 9 or 10, certainly less than a boy of puberty And in matters of judgment he is childish

This discrepancy between his judgment and his emotions on the one hand, and his intellectual attainments on the other, is a greater discrepancy than we find in normal persons

He seemed to be quite interested in describing the planning of this crime In the description of the crime itself he was extremely indifferent And in describing the pain he brought to the families involved he seemed quite indifferent He had no remorse He was interested in the crime as a technical thing He had no adequate emotional reaction to it

Richard got quite a kick out of discussing the crime with his family It pleased him that his mother should say to him that the criminal who had killed Robert Franks should be tarred and feathered

He was a little worried about his father's silence, afraid he might suspect something

Not purposely, but by chance, he passed the Franks home He experienced no remorse, except when he saw the coffin being brought out by the small, white-faced boys Then he felt a little bit uncomfortable

At no time has he dreamed about this crime Nor has his sleep been disturbed in any way

Their original plan with whatever boy they were to choose, was to strike him on the head with a taped chisel, being taped to protect the hand of the wielder, to take him to the culvert and there to strangle him Each of the two young men was to hold one end of the strangling rope Then to obliterate from the body all marks of identification and to place it in the culvert, where it was to remain forever, or until it had disintegrated

The witness next spoke of Leopold

In his religious studies he was intensely interested in classification, as he was in other things, too, and he finally found fault with God and as far as he was concerned he abolished God because God makes mistakes God made a great mistake when he took his mother, an almost perfect woman, and left others not so perfect

He then became an atheist At the university on the admission card he preferred to register "Atheist"

Leopold finally conceived life existing without any God and there being no God there is no right or wrong *per se* He said his mother's death changed his entire philosophy of life He seemed to lose inspiration and never did adjust himself normally to the world nor to himself thereafter

His tendency to classify things led him into a maze of fragments of philosophy from this author and that author His philosophical knowledge does not stand close scrutiny He thinks it does The net result is that he has abolished the ordinary classification which most of us accept as to what things are right and wrong

The Loeb-Leopold Case

Q What did he say to you as to his attitude toward friends?

A He has had no close friends. He has always desired a friend, but that friend must fit in, he felt, with that king-slave fantasy which has been the keynote of his inner mental life. He was very sensitive to the criticism of others. He preferred to live a non-emotional life, if he could. His ideal was a sheer intellectualist. His mood is more or less level, and rather shallow. He has no strongly developed emotions. His philosophy of life is that of sheer selfishness. He felt that the rules which hold ordinary men did not apply to him, because he was so superior. The only serious mistake he could make would be a mistake of intellect.

Q What were his reactions in jail as they appeared to you?

A In jail in discussing this crime, he took particular pains to be accurate. There was no other emotion of any kind, neither chagrin, remorse nor discomfort at being in jail, and no apprehension as to his future. I asked him what his plans were. He said, "Well I can't tell what my future will be, but I would prefer to get married and settle down."

Q Did you discuss with him the question of hanging?

A Yes. He said that the end of life is the end of all, that one might as well hang as not, and that if his family would feel bad about it, they should disown him before he should be hanged.

Q Did he show any emotional disturbance when you discussed the question of hanging with him?

A None that I could see.

Q Did he show any emotional disturbance when you discussed the Franks case with him?

A He denied any feeling of remorse, stated he had no feeling of having done anything morally wrong. He said he was disinclined to commit another such crime, not from a sense of remorse, but because it would be impossible to plan a perfect crime intellectually. He said he had no enjoyment, pleasure sorrow or grief from the crime.

Q What did he tell you was the motive for the Franks homicide and kidnaping?

The Loeb-Leopold Case

A It was a desire on the part of Richard Loeb to commit a perfect crime, and a desire on his part to do whatever Richard Loeb wanted him to do

Q What were your psychiatric observations so far as Nathan Leopold Jr, was concerned?

A He appears to have the intellect of a man thirty years of age who has been a student all his life. His mental development has been extremely precocious. One was next impressed by the disparity between his emotional poverty compared with his intellectual wealth, and the discrepancy between these two is extreme. One was greatly impressed by the vividness, the intensity, the duration and the characteristics of his fantasies and the effect of these fantasies in fashioning his personality was obvious. His judgment is that of a child.

His sense of inferiority, and the duel between that and the satisfying sense of superiority acquired from his intellectual development, showed an inner mental conflict of pathological importance.

His desire to classify things, to lead a nonemotional life, to be an intellectualist, was greater than we find in the average youth. His final opinion of himself as the supreme being of the world is definitely abnormal.

His lack of emotional feeling of any kind toward the crime is definite evidence of an abnormal mental state.

Q Referring to both the Loeb boy and the Leopold boy, I will ask you to state what you found with reference to their complementary relationship?

A Each boy felt inadequate to carry out the life he most desired unless he had some one else in his life to complement him, to complete him. Leopold on the one hand, wanted a superior for a companion. Loeb, on the other, wanted some one to adulate him for a companion.

The psychiatric cause for this is not to be found in either boy alone, but in the interplay of their two personalities, caused by their two constitutions and experiences. This friendship between the two boys was not altogether a pleasant one to either of them. The ideas that each proposed to the other were repulsive. Their friendship was not based so much on desire as on need, they being what they were.

Loeb did not crave the companionship of Leopold, nor did he respect him thoroughly. But he did feel the need of someone else in his life. Leopold did not like the faults, the criminalism of Loeb, but he did need someone in his life to carry out this king-slave compulsion.

Their emotions such as they had, were so diverse that they did not feel attracted to each other for their personality worth, nor did their emotions permit them to rebel against each other. They took each other somewhat as a matter of course.

Q Now, will you tell us what was the physical and neurological examination that you made of Leopold?

A There is to be found in Nathan Leopold, Jr., considerable pathology. The hair development is pronounced. The blood pressure was low. His eyes are somewhat prominent. One eyelid is lower than the other. His face is not the same on the two sides there being asymmetry. His heart sounds were clear, no disease of the lungs, some curvature of the spine. He is rather round shouldered. The abdomen protrudes. He is flat-footed. The thyroid gland may be felt. He has dermographia, or a disorder of the nervous control of the blood vessels. From all of which it was concluded, bearing the history in mind, that he has neuro-circulatory-asthenia, or vasomotor instability.

Q Give us in full the endocrine findings as to Leopold.

A From my examination and study of this and similar cases I believe that the thymus gland involuted unusually early, for the following reasons: his sexual maturity came on early, he had a very low resistance to infections, and there is a tendency to acidosis confirmed by low carbon dioxide, by his early permanent teeth, by his early secondary hair, his short body, stocky frame. The pineal gland has involuted early, because of the X-ray showing that it has already calcified at the age of 19, by the muscular fatigue, his mental precocity, the disorder in his blood, the sugar disturbance, the thyroid gland has been definitely diseased, that it has been an over-active thyroid, that the over-activity has now subsided, because of the definite history of a rapid pulse, by the condition of the skin, which is thick and dry, with coarse hair, by his large teeth and their poor condition, by his slow pulse now, by his low temperature, low blood pressure, low metabolism rate, by his mild anemia, his early sex development, by his skin reactions, dermographia, by his sugar intolerance He has a disorder of the adrenal glands, medullary insufficiency I have come to the conclusion that his sex glands are over functioning, because of his short, stocky build his early and complete sexual development in both primary and secondary characteristics, and the strong sex urge

Q What relation is there between the abnormal functioning of his endocrine glands and his mental condition?

A The effect of the endocrine glands on the mental condition is definitely established in the minds of medical men in certain points and is still a matter of dispute in others But I would say that his endocrine disorder is responsible for the following mental findings his precocious mental development, his rapid advance through school, his ease of learning, are of endocrine origin The fact that the cruel instincts show but little inhibition, is of endocrine origin The fact that his mental habits are fixed early in life, is of endocrine origin That his mind and body are everlastingly busy is of endocrine origin That he fatigues if he overexerts himself and is nonaggressive the prey of hidden fears, neurotic and unmoral, and at the same time keen and witty, is of endocrine origin The early development and strength of his sex urge is obviously of endocrine origin His shallow mood and his good bearing are of endocrine origin

Q Now, you refer to intellectual precocity taking place at a very early age, and a drive forward of that tendency?

A Yes

Q What would be the effect of that upon him, where there was not a corresponding maturity of his emotional life and his judgment?

A The effect of the intellectual drive of endocrine origin judgment immaturity, and emotional shallowness, is that he now has mentally a decided degree of discrepancy, a diseased discrepancy between his judgment and emotions on the one hand, and his intellect on the other hand

Q Mr Crowe asked you whether the number of sweethearts that Richard Loeb had would not indicate a depth of emotion I will ask you now to state whether or not the large number would not indicate a shallowness of emotion

A It depends upon whether he had them all at one time If he had many sweethearts all at one time, his emotions of course were shallow The man who truly loves his sweetheart has no room in his heart for anyone else at that time

Mr Crowe Doctor, may I interrupt, are you also an expert on love and love-making?

The Witness Only in so far as it has neuro-psychiatric importance

Mr Crowe Now doctor, you do not think very much of Loeb's judgment, do you?

A No, sir

Q Will you give me some illustration of his lack of judgment?

A Yes, sir The greatest illustration is that he, a boy with opportunities far higher than the average boy in Chicago, would engage himself in a life which was definitely doomed to destruction

Q Well, that is the crime itself

A Yes, that is the best example of defective judgment that I can find in him

Q Loeb is a very restless fellow, isn't he?

A Sometimes, yes sir

Q But not all the time?

A No, sir He would even go to sleep in the examining room while I was talking to the other patient

Q Well, a man who can go to sleep while a doctor is examining his companion's mental condition is not an extremely restless person, is he?

A Not at the time he is asleep of course not I think Loeb showed poor judgment in selecting the courses he took at college He said he drifted through college, following the line of least resistance That is poor judgment Any man that wants to study law as he had planned to do should prepare himself as very best he can.

Q Now, General Grant, in his life of himself states that when he went through West Point he spent most of his time reading Charlie Lever's novels and just slid through. Was that a case of poor judgment on Grant's part?

A It was.

Dr. Hugh T. Patrick was the first witness called by the State in rebuttal. He said that the defendants were not without emotional reactions and gave a number of examples from his own observations and from a consideration of the Bowman-Hulbert report. He found, he said, no evidence of mental disease.

Dr. Archibald Church, next called as a witness for the State, testified that upon observation he had seen no evidence of mental disease in either defendant. A number of questions were asked him on cross-examination.

Mr. Darrow What do you mean by an emotion?

Dr. Church Emotion is a play of feeling.

Q There is a difference between the part of the human anatomy which produces emotion and the mind, which is supposed to be the seat of reason, isn't there?

A I don't know of any such difference. No one has emotion unless he intellectually perceives it.

Q You are assuming that mind is the product of brain action?

A Yes, I believe it.

Q The mind is probably a product of the whole organism, isn't it?

A No, I don't think so.

Q Is there anything in the mind excepting the manifestations of the physical organization?

The Loeb-Leopold Case

A Practically not

Q Are there various centers in the brain for certain emotions?

A Not as far as I know. There are some who place sexual emotions in the cerebellum and others who place certain moral emotions in the large ganglia at the base, but as far as I know, there is no confirmation of those localizations

Q Is it correct to say moral emotions?

A Well, that is descriptive of one variety of emotional action, those which pertain to the duties and obligations between men

Q Where does one get those?

A They are usually a matter of experience or education. The ethical ideas must always be instilled in a child, because the only two emotions which he has at birth are fear of sound and fear from a sense of falling

Q The whole idea of moral emotions is built up from teachings, is it not?

A Precept and example

Q And the strength of the precept and the example and the teaching as compared with the primitive emotions determines the conduct, doesn't it?

A Yes, I think those things are related

Q That is, if the teaching is deep enough and the habit is strong enough, people will stay in the moral groove. And if the emotions are so strong and the teachings are so weak, they may leap over it?

A Yes. It is a question of self-control, which turns again upon the question of discipline

Q Self-control means pure discipline, doesn't it?

A Yes

Q So the whole question of education, what we call moral education, is a question of fixing habit deep into the individual so that he will withstand temptation?

A Yes, I think so

Q When is the most trying age in a young man?

A At the age of puberty and adolescence

Q Then comes a change of emotional life, doesn't it, as a rule?

The Loeb-Leopold Case

A Yes, sir

Q Then, if ever with the young man or the young woman they are the most apt to jump out of or leave the habits that have been inculcated in them to keep in a given path and break over on account of new feelings or emotions, are they not?

A They are. We are all familiar with the swell-head of youth.

Q And it is the most prolific time for insanity with youth, is it not?

A Yes

Q Do one's beliefs and theories of action or theories of life ever affect his conduct?

A Oh yes

Q Well, doctor, Leopold's views as to religion seemed very thoroughly fixed, did they not?

A I thought so

Q As to the superman did you go into it enough to know whether those were firmly fixed?

A No

Q How far one's conduct might be influenced by his views would depend a good deal upon the strength and permanency of them, would it not?

A It would

Q And that you could not give an opinion on in this case?

A No excepting as to his attitude on religion

Q You know something about dreams?

A Yes I regularly inquire into the character of dreams in nervous people. According to Freud they are a very good index of character. I do not follow Freud to that degree.

Q Do you follow him to any extent?

A No. The character of the dreams, whether pleasurable or unpleasurable, has for me a significance as a reflex of the physical condition, but the content of the dream to my mind is of very little significance.

Q Do fantasies have anything to do in diagnoses?

A Yes I think fantasies have a significance in regard to character

The Loeb-Leopold Case

Q Did you examine for any in this case?
A No
Q Fantasies are carried over into real life?
A As long as they remain fantasies the individual knows their nature, that they are dreams or aspirations, and he may try to live up to them. In that way they modify conduct.
Q A diseased mind functions in fantasies often, doesn't it?
A I presume it does
Q And the individual is ruled by fantasies as well as realities often, is he not?
A Not until they attain the delusional stage
Q What is the difference between fantasy and delusion?
A Delusion is an error of judgment which the patient cannot correct under any circumstances, and fantasy is a dream which he realizes is a fantasy or a dream
Q You mean he can correct a fantasy but he cannot correct a delusion?
A Yes
Q As a broad general rule, a daydream and a night dream are both reflections of mental life?
A Nothing can occur in a fantasy or in a night dream that has not in some way come to the experience of the individual
Q If you would know all a man's dreams, or a boy's dreams, and fantasies, and hopes, and ideals you would know something about the boy would you not?
A You would know the boy's character

Dr Harold D Singer was the next witness for the State. His conclusion was that neither Loeb nor Leopold was afflicted with any mental disease and he stated, in response to a question, that a paranoid personality was not a disease. Following is a part of the cross-examination by Mr Darrow

Q What is a split personality?
A A splitting in the personality is the separation of cer-

tain emotional experiences which for some reason are repressed out of consciousness and are difficult to recall In some of the disease conditions it seems that one can not recall them In nondisease conditions it is possible to recall them

Q That is the normal mind generally flows along a regular channel altogether, does it not?

A I could not answer that I don't know what a normal mind is even It is a hypothesis

Q Yes Well, then, of course you do not know whether these boys have a normal mind or an abnormal mind Is that right?

A I say they have a mind that is within the range of the normal

Q If I fail to remember a name, is that an indication of split personality?

A Yes, sir of a splitting off of a certain probably small experience in your life

Q Is it not just an indication that it did not impress itself strongly enough on me so I can recall it?

A It may be an evidence of senility and that the nerve pathways are undergoing degeneration

Q It might in me, but how with you?

A It might even in me

Q You have known of cases in the institutions like a woman confined there as a scrub woman who thinks she is the Queen of Sheba, haven't you?

A I don't recall that particular instance, but something similar to that

Q Yes Is that a question of split personality?

A In one sense, perhaps, and in another sense, no, but a good many of them are

Q If I say I am feeling like John L Sullivan this morning, that does not mean I think I am John L Sullivan

A That would be just the distinction between whether it was an evidence of mental disease or not

Q But if I said I was John L Sullivan, and John L Sullivan come back to life and wanting to challenge Dempsey, that would be different?

The Loeb-Leopold Case

A I would probably be able to sign a certificate on that ground

Q Now if a woman who is a scrub woman in an institution says she is the Queen of Sheba, that is a different thing, isn't it?

A I don't see that that is much different from the assumption about yourself

Q Maybe I have got it

A Maybe you have, but I have not seen any evidence of it yet

Dr Rollin T Woodyatt was the next State witness He stated that the general status of knowledge concerning the endocrine glands might almost " be compared to the interior of Africa before Stanley went there " He said " There are many definite facts known, but they are scattered, disordered, unrelated This field of endocrinology beyond the coastline of definite information is a field which has been exploited by romantic writers, charlatans, and others who are not to be classified as scientists "

To many of the questions asked the witness on cross-examination his reply was, " I don't know " A visiting lawyer remarked, " I can die cheerfully now, at last I have heard a medical expert who isn't afraid to say, ' I don't know.' "

Dr W O Krohn was next called as a witness by the State The following points, he said, built up the evidence of no mental disease in Loeb

Health and integrity of memory, as shown by his ability to tell the details of the fake alibi, and the details of the planning of the crime

Judgment, as illustrated by the way he told the officials that he had been driving and had not struck the fatal blows

The same type of judgment was operative in his evaluation of moral conditions

Logical sequence of the entire story

Every answer was responsive

Excellence of attention during the interview in the State's Attorney's office

Good reasoning by deduction

Of Leopold the witness gave a similar opinion; he saw nothing indicating mental disease. He stressed as factors helping to form his opinion

Remarkable memory, especially with regard to the books he had read and subjects studied

Not a single break in logic

Not a single skip in the chain of facts that he marshaled in his support of his argument that he was driving the car and Loeb struck the blow

Extreme courtesy to others in little things, showing that a man so regardful in small matters would certainly have mental power and capacity to be regardful of the rights of others in larger matters

Perfectly oriented as to time, space, and social relations

At the conclusion of the evidence arguments were made to the court by District Attorney Robert E. Crowe and Assistant District Attorneys Thomas Marshall and Joseph P. Savage for the State, and by Walter Bachrach, Clarence Darrow and Benjamin C. Bachrach for the defense. All of these arguments are given here in the order of their delivery. Perhaps it should be stated, in fairness and accuracy, that many pages, from almost as many books, both legal and medical, were read by some of the counsel on either side in connection with their arguments, but which, though more or less relevant there, have been, in part, omitted here — none being found in the following pages save such as were thought would prove of interest to the reader and of maybe more than mercurial value.

Speech of Thomas Marshall

IF THE COURT PLEASE

THERE is in this case but one question before the court. What punishment is proportionate to the turpitude of the offense?

If this is not a murder of the extreme type on the facts, then, of course, a lesser penalty than death can be invoked, but when months of planning, careful execution of every detail, a money motive, a kidnaping for ransom, the cruel blows of a sharp steel chisel, the gagging, the death, and the hiding of the body all appear, as they do here, the malice and deliberation take the crime out of the scale of lesser penalties and prescribe death

The statute, it is true, ranges from fourteen years to the death penalty, and the court has a duty to fix a penalty that is proportionate to the depravity and the viciousness of the crime committed, and in arriving at its decision here, the court must exercise a discretion Not a personal, arbitrary, willful discretion, but a judicial discretion; the application of the law to the existing facts Twice over under the statutes of the State the death penalty is provided by law under these facts and the State insists that any lesser penalty would violate both the spirit and the letter of the law

As was said by Chief Justice Marshall, in *Osborne vs U S Bank, 22 U S , 738·*

Courts are the mere instruments of the law, and can will nothing When they are said to exercise a discretion it is a mere legal discretion, a discretion to be exercised in discerning the course prescribed by law, and, when that is discerned, it is the duty of the court to follow it Judicial power is never exercised for the purpose of giving effect to the will of the judge, always for the purpose of giving effect to the will of the legislature, or, in other words, to the will of the law

If your Honor please, this is a government of laws and not of men Here in this court all are on a perfect equality The poor and the rich, the learned and the unlettered. No man is above the law, and none beyond its reach Every officer of the law is himself within the law, and the uniform enforcement of the law is the strength and security of the State

As I understand this legal situation, three things are involved in any decision of the one major question in the case In determining punishment the court must consider, first, responsibility, second, mitigation, if any exists, and third, turpitude

Responsibility is a condition, a status There

are no grades or degrees. One is either responsible or not responsible, and in this case the responsibility is admitted by the pleas of guilty. It is proved by the confessions and by the evidence in the case and it is repeatedly insisted upon by the assertions and arguments of the defendants' counsel

Now, if Loeb and Leopold are responsible enough to receive a sentence to the penitentiary, they are responsible enough for the extreme penalty. The measure of responsibility is the same in either case.

I wish to read the following extract from the *Wireback* case, *190 Pennsylvania, 138*

> He continues to be a legitimate subject of punishment, although he may be laboring under a moral obliquity of perception as much as if he were merely laboring under an obliquity of vision. There is no middle ground which the law recognizes, nor does a doubt of sanity reduce the grade of the crime to murder in the second degree. From the very nature of mental disease there can be no grading of it by degrees so as to accord with the degree of the crime

That is the law in every jurisdiction. We have the same responsibility here, legal responsibility, whether the punishment be fourteen years in the penitentiary, or life, or the extreme penalty of death on the gallows.

In *Hogue vs State, 65 Texas Criminal, 539*, it was said.

> This court has never recognized the doctrine that a person with a mind below the normal should not be

found guilty and punished, and the only relief for any person of an insane mind, under our statute, is that if such person is incapable of knowing and understanding the act, when committed, to be wrong, he is not susceptible to any punishment. It would be a strange spectacle if the courts were permitted to speculate as to the degree of intelligence existing in the mind of a person charged with crime, unless some limitation or point was reached where culpability ceased, and when that point was reached he was not culpable.

If there is no responsibility here, there can be no punishment at all. But if there can be punishment, then the matter of their mental disease, their phantasies, their delusions, their hallucinations, all that structure upon which days have been spent, is of no avail.

The turpitude of the offense still remains as it was. It stands here an aggravated murder, a helpless, defenseless little boy, lured into this automobile by these fiendish-minded men, slain with the blows of this cold chisel.

What for? The money motive. They kidnaped him for ransom, $10,000 in old bills, *throw it from a train*, stealing a typewriter way back here months before, carefully planned, every detail looked after.

Any mitigation shown? Phantasies, hallucinations and delusions that go to responsibility only, and nothing whatever that affects the turpitude of the crime. And they have been beside the mark, because it is upon the turpitude of the crime that the court is required by the law of the land to fix the punishment

Mr Darrow Turpitude of the party, isn't it? The word turpitude doesn't attach to an act, does it?

Mr Marshall It characterizes it or describes it

Mr Darrow It describes the person, doesn't it?

Mr Marshall There is in this case not even a reasonable doubt of the sanity of these defendants because that is included in the plea of guilty That covers the whole field of responsibility, and leaves open entirely and with no evidence in mitigation before the court, the facts and circumstances, the viciousness, the depravity, in the language of the Supreme Court, the " turpitude " of the act itself

Now, as a tangent to this responsibility, we have it in evidence in the case that Leopold, Jr , asserted himself to be a superman, believed that he was above the law, that if he thought it right to commit a murder, then so far as he was concerned it was right This was his philosophy, based upon his views of the Nietzschean doctrines

Your Honor, we have had in this State one outstanding great criminal trial prior to this one I refer to the Anarchists Case The anarchists also had their philosophy

Following are extracts from some of their speeches

All governments are domineering parties Assassination will remove the evil from the face of the earth For freedom all things are just

We need no president, no congressmen, no police, no militia, no judges They are all leeches sucking the blood of the poor who have to support them by their labor

We are told that we must obtain our means and need by obeying law and order Damn law and order We have obeyed law and order long enough The time has come for you men to strangle the law or the law will strangle you

That was the philosophy of the anarchists, to destroy the law The philosophy here is that the law has no application The anarchists believed in their doctrine of social revolution, but they were executed under the laws that they damned, executed not for their abstract opinions, not for their theory and philosophy, but because of their murder Mistaken men that they were, they had no selfish money motive for their crime

Only so recently as *People vs Lloyd et al, 304 Illinois, 23*, the communists also had a philosophy and a theory of revolutionary socialism They aimed to conquer the power of the State They were convicted of a conspiracy and their conviction affirmed in the Supreme Court.'

Upon what theory can it be said that the views of Leopold, Jr, his philosophy and his opinions, if they do not protect him against the law itself and his punishment, can in any wise be urged in mitigation?

This whole question has been before the Supreme Court of the United States, growing out of the religious beliefs of the Mormons. Their church required of them that where possible they practice polygamy. But Congress made polygamy punishable. The question went to the Supreme Court upon conviction of one Reynolds in the then territory of Utah. In *Reynolds vs United States, 98 U S Supreme Court Reports, 145*, in an opinion by Mr. Chief Justice White, it is said

> On the trial accused proved that at the time of his alleged second marriage, and for many years before, he had been a member of the Church of Jesus Christ of Latter-Day Saints commonly called the Mormon Church, and a believer in its doctrines, that it was the duty of the male members of said church, circumstances permitting, to practice polygamy, that members of the church believed that the practice of polygamy was directly enjoined upon the male members thereof by Almighty God, in a revelation to Joseph Smith, the founder and prophet of said church and that the penalty for failing or refusing to do so would be damnation in the life to come
>
> In our opinion the statute immediately under consideration is within the legislative power of Congress It is constitutional and valid as prescribing a rule of action for all those residing in the territories and places over which the United States has exclusive control This being so, the only question which remains is,

whether those who make polygamy a part of religion are excepted from the operation of the statute If they are, then those who do not make polygamy a part of their religious belief may be found guilty and punished, while those who do must be acquitted and go free This would be introducing a new element into criminal law Laws are made for the government of actions, and while they cannot interfere with mere religious belief and opinions, they may with practices Suppose one believed that human sacrifices were a necessary part of religious worship, would it be seriously contended that the civil government under which he lived could not interfere to prevent a sacrifice? Or if a wife religiously believed that it was her duty to burn herself on the funeral pile of her dead husband, would it be beyond the power of the civil government to prevent her carrying her belief into practice?

So here, as the law of the organization of society under the exclusive dominion of the United States, it is provided that plural marriages shall not be allowed Can a man excuse his practices to the contrary because of his religious belief? To permit this would be to make the professed doctrines of religious belief superior to the law of the land, and in effect permit every citizen to become a law unto himself Government could exist only in name under such circumstances

Our position is, your Honor, first, that these defendants are, within the meaning of the law, responsible for their crimes, second, that weak-mindedness or mental disease is not to be accepted in mitigation, and, third, that the punishment under the law is to be proportionate to the turpitude of the offense

The Loeb-Leopold Case

Our statute says that murder is the unlawful killing of a human being, in the peace of the People, by a person of sound mind, with malice aforethought, either express or implied. Our Supreme Court says that one is in the peace of the People when he has not forfeited the right to live.

Was Robert Franks "in the peace of the People"? Your Honor, all the elements of the crime are here — and admitted. Responsibility, malice, deliberation — all are here. Is it a case that merits the extreme penalty or a lesser crime that falls within the lesser penalties of the statute?

What are the facts? Loeb and Leopold composed a letter for any case as it might arise. They prepared a form letter, to have it ready. They wrote the ransom letter and rewrote it. It was a finished job. All it needed was the filling in of the name, and mailing it.

Then they arranged for the death car, assuming the name of Morton D. Ballard, renting a room at the Morrison Hotel, merely for the purpose of providing for a place to receive the identification card, going down to the Rent-a-Car people, giving a wrong name, getting the recommendation from "Mason" over the telephone — and Loeb on the telephone giving Leopold a good character.

They bought the hydrochloric acid, they bought the cold chisel, they taped it, they bought the pieces of rope and got the cloth for a gag and had a lap robe there to carry the body.

The Loeb-Leopold Case

They planned first to pick up young Levinson They went down to the school They looked up the telephone book for Levinson's address The Levinson boy was gone when they got back They waited an hour or so, and then got field glasses that they might spy out the boy they were picking out to murder The boy went down the alley, and they lost track of him They went to Levinson's home, but did not see him On the way back the fates so had it that they saw the Franks boy They at once decided to kidnap him

These two stalwart youths, two full-grown persons if you please, inveigled the little boy into the car, and then one of them — and they each disclaim and accuse the other — struck the Franks boy with the chisel, and dragged him over the back of the seat The coroner's physician tells us that there were four gashes on the head of that boy, and the evidence shows much blood

They drove south to the Midway, and stopped to telephone a young lady, and to get something to eat The boy was dead When he was pulled back into the back of the car he had made noises, and rags were stuffed in his mouth Then they went to the culvert and disrobed the body, and Leopold poured the hydrochloric acid over the face Remember the debate between these two men before they selected hydrochloric acid? One thought it should be sulphuric, and the other said hydrochloric

Then they put away the body in the culvert, after they poured the acid over the face And the things that they took away were burned at Loeb's home, except the shoes, belt and blanket They burned the blanket elsewhere, and disposed of the shoes, and then mailed this ransom letter

They had to kill the boy because the boy knew them, and would identify them Their plan at the outset was to kill the boy to carry through the ransom program, and when they mailed the ransom letter the boy was dead and in the culvert. They washed out the car and told the chauffeur the blood was wine, and then they returned the car to the owner, throwing away the chisel Then they planted a letter in the Pullman car and they sent Franks instructions about taking a train, and they sent a cab to the house

"Put $10,000 in a cigar box in old bills and throw it off the train," and Loeb and Leopold would be on hand to pick up the money, but if the train slowed down, or anything happened, they would know it, and they could get away

It is proved here that they wanted to commit the master crime, they wanted to talk about it and read about it. The master criminals wanted to commit the perfect crime that could not be detected They did commit a most atrocious crime, and went about it with deliberation and a malice aforethought that carries with it only one punishment, and that is the extreme penalty.

The Loeb-Leopold Case

There is a young man, your Honor, nineteen years of age, in the county jail at the present moment, Bernard Grant, under a sentence of death. Grant went into a store to commit a robbery, and in the course of that robbery there was a struggle with the police officer, who was killed. There was perhaps no original intention to commit the murder.

Shall Grant go to the gallows, under the law, when men of the same age, of greater education, of better opportunity, can deliberately plan and scheme a murder and kidnaping for ransom for months and months, carry it into execution and by any possibility escape that penalty?

In *People vs Savant, 301 Illinois, 225*, the sentence of death upon John Savant was upheld. Savant is executed under the laws of the State and he was acting on the belief that the man he killed was intimate with his wife, and when he spoke to him the man laughed at him, and he killed him. Compare the turpitude in such a case with that found here — two capital crimes interwoven!

I wondered when I read this case as to Savant whether he was six or eight years of age by the Binet-Simon tests. At any rate, he was old enough to know the law and he was old enough to suffer the penalty of death. There was not any extensive plan in Savant's case. There was not any preparation. There was not a kidnaping for ransom, no buying of chisels and hydrochloric acid, but the turpitude was sufficient to take Savant to the gallows

In 1908, David Anderson, nineteen years of age, was sentenced to death in Cook County for murder It was the shooting on the street of a police officer under a chance meeting, with such malice as goes with that kind of a killing, of course, but with no extended premeditation such as we have here Yet, Anderson, at nineteen years of age, upon a conviction in this court, was sentenced to die

Mr B C Bachrach. Mr Marshall, you know that it was commuted to life because he was only nineteen?

Mr Marshall I am not discussing that phase at all What other agencies do is beyond us This is a court

Mr Darrow That was not a hearing before a court on a plea of guilty, it was a jury trial

Mr Marshall But where lies the difference between a jury trial and a plea of guilty? All that you have in mitigation and all that the State has in aggravation goes into the record on a jury trial

Mr Darrow It doesn't mean they are decided the same way, a court and a jury

Mr Marshall It is the same decision whether it be through a jury or as here upon your plea It amounts to a conviction upon the record, and, if you please, a conviction of the highest order

Anderson did not plan that killing of that police officer for months. That group went down the street, they met the officer, were accosted, and shots were fired, the officer is dead, and Anderson is sentenced by the court to the death penalty, and it is affirmed in the Supreme Court. If we have governors who interfere with the courts, that is the executive branch of the government, and not the judicial. If the courts do their duty, their whole responsibility is ended. Let the judiciary assume and accept the responsibility for their acts.

Mr Darrow: Wouldn't the jury have been justified in sentencing him to life there?

Mr Marshall: I think not. I think with the Supreme Court in such a case.

Mr Darrow: The Supreme Court didn't say that the jury would not have been justified in sending him to the penitentiary for life.

Mr Marshall: They say the judgment is affirmed, do they not?

Mr Darrow: That is all they say.

Mr Marshall: If the court please, I wish to refer here to a list of executions in Cook County for some years past, giving the ages of the defendants. Richard G. Ivens, twenty-four years of age, Andrew Williams, twenty-two, Frank Shiblawski, twenty-two, Ewald Shiblawski, twenty-three, Thomas Schultz, nineteen, Philip Sommerling, thirty, Dennis Anderson, twenty-one, Albert Johnson, twenty-five, Earl Dear, twenty-six, John O'Brien, twenty-two, William Yancey Mills, twenty-one, Lloyd Bopp, twenty-three, Frank Camponi and Frank Zager, twenty-two, each of them, Nicholas Viani was seventeen years old when he was convicted, eighteen when he was executed, Oscar McCavit was twenty-three, Harvey Church was twenty-three

These men named have all been executed, and at the present time, in jail, awaiting the day of execution, are Walter Krauser, twenty-one, and Bernard Grant, nineteen

If youth is to mitigate an atrocious murder, if age is to save these men from their just punishment, every conviction that I have cited that has led to the gallows has been a mistake in the law, because not one of them — and I know something of the facts in each of them — not one of them compares in premeditation, in malice or in execution with the terrible crime that is here for judgment

Take this seventeen-year-old murderer, Nicholas Viani, eighteen when he was executed

This crime, when laid parallel with the record in this case as it is here before the court, is a simple crime indeed Viani, with his companions, ran into a saloon, fired on the owner, took his money and went out Viani was young and had been led into crime but, none the less, his responsibility under the law was complete and he was executed

This is not the only case, your Honor that has ever come in on a plea Before Judge Kavanaugh, in this court, James Smith and James Butler on

January 16, 1923, pleaded guilty to an indictment upon a charge of murder and to each of them testimony was heard in part but continued, and on the 17th of January, the next day after the plea, Butler was sent to the penitentiary for life and Smith was sentenced to execution

In the case of *People vs Haensell, 293 Illinois, 33,* there was an insanity defense Haensell was a soldier who had had various adventures He had had a blow on the head as a young man, had a goiter, had syphilis, and presented the defense that he was insane He received treatment for three and a half months in the hospital for goiter and vertigo, after which he was honorably discharged from the army as unfit for overseas duty He returned to Chicago He complained to the police that his wife and his mother were entertaining soldiers at the mother's home He later killed both

Conviction on an insanity defense, which may have had a real basis, for all I know, not phantasies, not delusions, but something of substance, certainly the conditions recited give some foundation for the assumption that there was something there, and yet over against that, he was not mentally diseased enough to escape the gallows.

Here is another conviction and execution, *People vs Laures, 289 Illinois, 490* He was convicted for the murder of Celestino Blanco The defendant was engaged to marry one Josephina Alvarez, who kept a boarding house. The deceased boarded at her

The Loeb-Leopold Case

home. This was the cause of strained relations, and, one day, the defendant shot and killed Blanco

The turpitude there was sufficient to take the defendant to the gallows Parallel that with this case There was no kidnaping for ransom, no $10,000 in old bills to be thrown from a train, no killing of a small schoolboy, and telling his parents, in all their anxiety, that the boy was safe and sound, knowing all the time that the mutilated body was out in the tile pipe, its face eaten with acid There was no planning, no stolen typewriter, no taped chisel, no preparing and writing over of a ransom letter in that case, but it was just a case of passion

Your Honor, the books are full of such cases But nowhere will you find a case more terrible, more cunningly planned, more carefully executed, more dastardly than this case at bar

I shall give to your Honor a list, if I may, and serve counsel on the other side with the same, of these cases, and the others from the list, where the sentence of death has been affirmed in this State And I challenge counsel to point out in any of these cases a single one that nearly approaches in horror or atrocity, in fiendish depravity, the case that is before this court

I wish now, your Honor, to read from a learned decision in the case of *State vs Junkins, 147 Iowa, 588*, very appropriate here

In submitting the appeal to this court, counsel concede the guilt of the accused and admit that his conviction of the crime is sustained by the overwhelming weight of the testimony

Their plea for interference by this court is confined to the punishment assessed by the jury, which we were asked to reduce or change to imprisonment for life

The argument, presented with great earnestness and force, is that the appellant has been shown to be a degenerate whose defective mental and moral nature renders him no more responsible for manifestations of criminal violence than is a member of the brute creation having neither reason nor capacity to understand the moral quality of his acts

To take the life of such a person in vindication of law and order is said to be an idle act, for it cannot operate as a deterrent to others of his class, for such as he are the blind slaves of their abnormal passions and criminal tendencies, and when these are aroused to activity the possibility of punishment, however severe or drastic, will not suffice to turn them from their evil purpose

If a man who has led an honorable and law-abiding life becomes insane, and under the influence of a diseased mind commits an atrocious murder, the law does not demand his life in punishment but contents itself with putting him in confinement, by which to restrain him from other acts of violence

"If, then," says counsel, "the law interpose the shield of its protection to save the life of a once normal person who has become insane, why should we not be equally reluctant to pronounce the death penalty upon one, who, by reason of a defective organization, molded by prenatal limitations and conditions, and developed in vicious environment for which he is not responsible, is also incapable of appreciating moral or social obligations?"

The Loeb-Leopold Case

Counsel here touch upon a question which is having the increasing attention of students of criminology and kindred topics, and it may be true, as many learned investigators think, that the methods which now prevail of protecting society against its defective and criminal classes are of unscientific conception and so ineffective in practice that a civilized people should discard them for other and saner schemes of retributive and preventive justice

But, as we have already suggested, the reform must come, if at all, through the lawmaking power, and until then the courts must administer the law as it is written

We have not gone, nor shall we in this opinion go minutely into the horrifying details of appellant's offense It is enough to say that in all the history of crime none more inexcusable was ever committed It was murder, brutal, cruel, hideous, and cowardly in the extreme, and assuming the appellant's moral and legal responsibility, the assessment of anything less than the highest punishment provided by law would be a startling failure of justice

It may be, as counsel suggest, that he is the natural and inevitable product of 'Smoky Row' and the slums of the city and that in a certain sense the ultimate responsibility for turning out such as he to prey upon the innocent and helpless rests upon society or the State which permits, if not legalizes, the conditions which alone make such crimes possible, but the development of the ideal state in which crime shall be banished or destroyed by eliminating the causes which produce it is beyond our reach As now constituted, the law ordinarily observes only the overt criminal act of the rational individual and punishes it without attempting to trace the criminal impulse or inclination to its origin People are born and reared under circumstances varying from wealth, comfort, and wholesome example and influence on the one hand, to poverty, misery, and surroundings of the most unfavorable and corrupting character on the other, but all are made subject to the same law, and each must render to it the same measure of obedience. This is so because such are our human limitations that a finer discrimination and a juster apportionment of responsibility is apparently impossible, until we have reached a higher plane of civilization than has yet been achieved.

In conclusion, then, if your Honor please, I want to call your attention particularly to the language of the Iowa court where it characterized that murder as a cowardly murder, and I ask this court to contemplate the record here before you with that thought in mind.

Could anything be more cowardly, more terribly cowardly than the crime that was committed here? A fourteen-year-old helpless schoolboy lured by deceit into the automobile, by two stout, robust young men, bent upon murder, bent upon kidnaping for ransom, for ten thousand dollars in old bills, lured into that car, seated in the front seat to talk about a tennis racket with his friend, whom he had known for a long time, and while he is facing forward in that car, he is beaten upon the head with a steel chisel, and his life crushed out — a helpless boy. Cowardly? There is nothing in Illinois jurisprudence that compares with it.

And so, upon the whole of the record, compare all of the Illinois cases I have cited from the beginning down to this moment, and nowhere in any of them will you find the premeditation, the deliberate malice, the cunning plans, the months of preparation, the thought, the science, the ability

None of these things are to be found in the books in connection with the crime of murder, and here we have it in connection with two of the three highest crimes in the statute, the only two crimes in the State that are provided by the law with the death penalty — murder and kidnaping

The authorities construing those statutes say that the punishment under those statutes shall be proportionate to the turpitude of the offense All three elements are here, responsibility, aggravation beyond anything in the books anywhere, and no mitigation

There is only one sentence that can be imposed upon these vile culprits that fits the act they committed, yea, the acts they committed

Twice over the law requires their lives upon their admissions of record in this court, and any lesser penalty than the extreme penalty, upon the record in this case, would make a mockery of the law itself

I thank your Honor for the patience you have shown me

The Loeb-Leopold Case

Speech of Joseph P Savage

MAY IT PLEASE THE COURT AND COUNSEL FOR THE DEFENSE:

YOU have before you, your Honor, one of the most cold-blooded, cruel, and cowardly crimes ever committed in history

The evidence shows that some time during the month of November, 1923, Richard Loeb and Nathan Leopold went to Ann Arbor, Michigan, to attend a football game, Loeb and Leopold both having been former students of Michigan University, and Loeb being one of its youngest graduates

From the house of Loeb's fraternity they stole some gold pins, a few watches, a little money, and a typewriter These conspirators and intellectual murderers knew that if they were to purchase a typewriter here in Chicago, it would be possible to trace that typewriter to the owner, and they were taking no chance

After returning to Chicago, they began to look around, and to consider who their likely prospects might be for this dastardly crime

Among those they considered was young Billie Deutsch, the grandson of Julius Rosenwald, but, upon second consideration, Loeb, this boy who has no emotion, as they tried to argue to the court, thought that as his father was the vice president of Sears, Roebuck & Company and Julius Rosenwald, the president, it might be best to pick another boy.

Among others considered at that particular time was their bosom friend, Richard Rubel, this boy who, three times a week, would have lunch with both defendants. And they talked over just what method they would pursue to dispose of their companion, and then the thought came to them that if they had to dispose of Rubel some one might suspect them, also that Rubel's father was a tightwad, and in all probability would not come across with the cash

Their next move, your Honor, was to open a bank account, and Richard Loeb withdrew money from the bank and turned it over to Nathan Leopold so that he might open an account in the Hyde Park State Bank under the name of Morton D Ballard They next established a residence at the Morrison Hotel

Leopold then appeared at the Rent-a-Car Company and made application for a car, stating that he was a salesman from Peoria, and giving as his residence the Morrison Hotel, his bank account the Hyde Park State Bank, and as a city reference Louis Mason, 1352 Wabash Avenue Also the telephone number of the latter's store

Jacobs, the president of the concern called the telephone number that was given him by Leopold, who had represented himself as Morton D Ballard Loeb was awaiting the telephone call He answered the phone, and stated in response to the questions that were asked by Jacobs, the president, that his name was Mason, that he knew Ballard very well, and that he could recommend him very highly

It is fair to infer, your Honor, that the purpose of renting the car the first time was to establish their credit so that when they wanted to get the car at the opportune time, it would be easier

After having the car out two or three hours it was returned, and then the next step in this systematic planning of this horrible crime was to prepare to receive the money that they were about to demand from some one who at that time was unknown to them So Loeb, starting in some time in April, and continuing up until May 15th or 20th, would get on a Michigan Central train leaving the Illinois Central depot at 3 o'clock standard time, purchasing a ticket for Michigan City, taking the newspaper that they had specially prepared, and going to the rear of the platform, when the train would reach the vicinity of 74th and the Illinois Central tracks, where he would toss the package, while Leopold would watch to see where it would land

In every detail their plan was worked out, and they made approximately ten or twelve trips out on this train solely for the purpose of seeing where the money would land when they had consummated their plan and ordered the folks of their intended victim to throw the money in the designated spot

So that, on May 21st, 1924, Leopold, driving in his car, accompanied by Loeb, drove to the vicinity of 14th and Michigan Avenue There he left Loeb and entered the Rent-a-Car Company and purchased a ticket which entitled him to take a car, and making a fifty-dollar deposit

They had lunch at a restaurant located at Cottage Grove near Thirty-fifth, and after having their lunch, they put the curtains on this rented car that Leopold had obtained from the Rent-a-Car people They then left, Leopold driving his own car and Loeb driving the rented car

They drove to the vicinity of Forty-third and Cottage Grove Avenue, where Loeb left the car, went into a hardware store and purchased a chisel and rope, Leopold went to a drug store and there purchased a bottle of hydrochloric acid

And prior to that, your Honor, Leopold had gone to the stationery store, and there purchased envelopes and paper for the purpose of writing this letter, and this letter was carefully prepared in detail, leaving the envelope and letter unaddressed, they not knowing at that time who their victim might be

And with all their paraphernalia, with their chisel and rope and their letter, they then drove to the Leopold home Leopold entered the house and went into the bathroom, and there obtained from the medicine cabinet the tape that they were about to use on this chisel in this cold-blooded murder And while he was there he removed the boots that he knew would be necessary in placing the body of his intended victim in the culvert And the robe was

The Loeb-Leopold Case

taken from the house, and with the boots, robe, tape, automatic pistols, he left his home, to look for the victim

And then Loeb and Leopold drove to the Harvard School Loeb left the car and went into the yard, where he was well known by all the little boys in the neighborhood, and there he spoke to the tutor of Johnnie Levinson, that sweet, beautiful little boy who testified before your Honor, and who told you in all his innocence, that he talked to Loeb on that day, and God knows, when he was on this stand, he did not realize that he might have been the victim of this cruel, cold-blooded murder

And after talking to Johnnie Levinson, he entered the car, where Leopold was waiting for him, and then fearing that they might become observed in that vicinity and, one of the boys disappearing, that some one might suspect them, they decided to return to the Leopold home and get a pair of field glasses so they might observe their intended victim, and watch his movements, and at the same time not be observed themselves

After getting the field glasses at the Leopold home they returned to the Harvard School and from some distance they watched the little boys in that yard at play, and they watched in particular Johnnie Levinson And all at once the game broke up, and thinking that the boys who were running down the alley, still playing, were going to return again, they still remained And after waiting there a little while, and the boys not returning, they decided that they could possibly reach the Levinson boy's home before he could reach it. But they missed him.

They then started to drive around looking for some other victim. And while driving west on Forty-ninth Street, nearing Ellis Avenue, they saw Bobby Franks and immediately decided upon him. And this cold-blooded, fiendish murderer, if the court please, called to that little innocent boy, that undersized boy of fourteen years of age, who admired Richard Loeb, who played tennis in his yard day after day, called to him and said, "Bobby, don't you want a ride?" And Bobby thanked him and told him he would rather walk, only having a short distance to go.

And then what did the cowardly fiends do? Loeb says, "Come, Bobby, I want to introduce you to my friend Nathan Leopold," and as this manly little boy walked over and shook hands with Nathan Leopold on a further subterfuge to get this boy into the car, Loeb said he wanted to talk to him about his tennis racket. And then, oh, what then?

Why, Judge, you wouldn't strike a dog four times on the head with a chisel and not give him some chance.

Bobby Franks would have fought for his life, had he seen that blow coming. But no. The blow was struck from behind, that cowardly blow. And then, your Honor, counsel come here and cry out for mercy. What mercy did they show that boy? Why,

The Loeb-Leopold Case

after striking the four blows, they pulled him to the rear of the car and gouged his life out. Mercy? Your Honor, it is an insult in a case of this kind to come before the bar of justice and beg for mercy

Let us be just, before we are generous. I know your Honor will be just as merciful to these two defendants as they were to Bobby Franks

What chance did they give him for his life? And God knows his life would have been a life worth living, this gentlemanly little boy

Then they drove to the vicinity of 118th Street and the Panhandle tracks, they drove around and around waiting for it to become dark so that they might hide their victim without being seen

They stopped and had a sandwich, and while they were driving around, in the pocket of each of the murderers was a pistol. For what purpose? For the purpose of extinguishing the life of any pedestrian or citizen or police officer who might interfere

And when darkness came on, they took the body from this car and carried it in the blanket approximately two hundred feet. And then they removed the remainder of the clothes that this Franks boy had on, having taken his shoes, stockings and trousers off in the car, and after removing the boy's clothing Leopold removed his coat and shoes and put on his hip boots to keep his feet dry

Loeb took the bottle of hydrochloric acid from the car and proceeded to pour it on the face of Bobby Franks. Not satisfied with murdering the

The Loeb-Leopold Case

boy, they wanted to mutilate his body beyond recognition, so that that poor mother who resides on Ellis Avenue and that father who resides out there, and sisters and brothers, in years to come, would have never known the fate of the beloved boy

Leopold then, with his foot, pushed the body of the dead boy into the drain pipe

After placing the body there, he went up on the railroad tracks, where he started to remove the boots, and then called to his co-conspirator Loeb to hand him his coat, and when the coat was picked up was the time that the glasses dropped from his pocket

After placing the clothes of the little Franks boy in this blanket they went to the car and drove away

And while on the way in, your Honor, from this culvert, on this letter that they had prepared prior to this date, Leopold printed the name and address of Jacob Franks, marking it special, and continued on to the home of Loeb.

When they reached the home of Richard Loeb the clothing of the Franks boy was removed from the car, taken into the basement, and there they proceeded to burn the trousers, underwear, shirt and so forth of this little tot

And at this time, your Honor, to show you how cautious and how deliberate they were in their plans, they removed from the vest of this little boy his class pin, also his buckle and his belt, and they set aside his shoes because they knew that it was pos-

The Loeb-Leopold Case

sible that the shoes and the metals that they removed from the clothes of this boy would not burn

And when it came to the robe, which was saturated with blood at that time, Loeb hesitated about burning that robe in his home, because he feared that the stench might arouse suspicion in the house, or that it might create more smoke than usual and some one might become suspicious So they decided to take the robe and hide it out in the yard, and they did At this time Loeb secured a bucket of water and some soap, and they went out to where the car was standing, and in a half-hearted fashion they attempted to remove the blood from the car They next went to Leopold's home and parked the car

They then left the house and made a call They called the home of this little tot They asked for Mr Franks It was Mrs Franks who answered the phone It was at that time that Leopold told Mrs Franks " Your boy has been kidnaped He is safe Don't worry Instructions will follow later " And the boy was cold in death in that God-forsaken spot!

Can your Honor imagine how any one could call the mother of that little boy and tell her that? Can you imagine her feelings?

Then they continued on with their job The letter was mailed about twelve-thirty or one o'clock in the morning After perfecting their plans and carrying them as far forward as it was possible that night, Leopold then started to drive Loeb to his home. On the way home Loeb reached out of the car and tossed to the side that weapon that had crushed out the life of Bobby Franks, still wet with blood

And then they went on home I wonder, Judge, did they sleep well that night I wonder if that little boy's picture did not appear I wonder if they did not have a phantasy, a dream in which they saw Bobby Franks

The next day, your Honor, while the Franks family were awaiting this further word that they were informed they would receive they received that special delivery letter

It went on to tell them, if your Honor please, to secure ten thousand dollars in old bills, not marked, and how to prepare that package, and went on to tell them, your Honor, that any infraction of the instructions in that letter meant death for their boy

"A strictly commercial proposition "! Why, your Honor, they did not play the commercial proposition half straight They could have secured that ten thousand dollars without killing Bobby Franks They could have had that money, if they were desirous of having it, without shutting out the life of that little boy And the best proof of that, your Honor, is the fact that that morning when the bank opened, Jacob Franks appeared there and secured the ten thousand dollars, and then came on home and waited at that telephone, as he had been instructed to do in the letter

The Loeb-Leopold Case

That morning Leopold goes over to the University and Loeb meets him there, and about eleven o'clock they leave the University in Leopold's car and drive back to the home of Leopold

And, as your Honor well remembers, Englund, the Leopolds' chauffeur, the man who had never seen, prior to that time, Leopold touch his hands to a car, upon seeing those two washing out the car, came downstairs from his home above the garage and offered his assistance

Leopold stated that they had spilled some red wine on the carpet the night before and that Loeb did not want his father to see it, and when Englund offered to clean out the car, did they take any chances, your Honor? Oh, no They told him to go on back to the garage

After cleaning out the car they proceeded to the vicinity of the Illinois Central depot, where Loeb, as he had done many a time prior to this, your Honor, purchased a ticket for Michigan City With this other letter that they had prepared and addressed to Jacob Franks, in his pocket, he purchased a ticket to Michigan City and a seat in the car on that train, and he went into the train and while he was gone Leopold again called the home of Bobby Franks

And upon the phone being answered, he replied again "This is George Johnson," the same George Johnson who had advised him the night before that their boy had been kidnaped and was safe

He proceeded at once to give Jacob Franks instructions where to go with the ten thousand dollars He told him there would be a Yellow Cab at his door, and for him to get into the cab and go to the place named and there await a call

But Jacob Franks, five minutes prior to that time, your Honor, had learned his boy was murdered

He begged for time, he asked the supposed George Johnson on the other end of the line for a half hour longer But Leopold insisted that he go at once

They next called a Yellow Cab, and the order went to the Yellow Cab Company to send a cab to 5052 Ellis Avenue, the home of Jacob Franks, and that there was a load there waiting for them, and the cab was sent at once

After having placed this letter in the box that is used for blank telegrams, Loeb left the Pullman car, and when he got out on the street he tore up his pullman ticket and his railroad ticket which he had purchased and then he and Leopold started south They called the drug store that they had directed Jacob Franks to go to but Franks was not there

After trying to reach Jacob Franks twice in this drug store, they noticed a newspaper stand and on that stand in large headlines appeared the statement that the boy's body had been found

Leopold still insisted upon getting the ten thousand dollars, wanted to go on But Loeb, cool of judgment, insisted that if they continued to try and get the money after that boy's body had been found, they would be taking chances of being caught. So the plan was given up

And was it an elaborate plan, your Honor? This drug store was located about two hundred feet from the Illinois Central depot on 63rd Street It was their intention to have Jacob Franks go to this drug store, they would make their call there, nobody knew what instructions he would receive, consequently the police could not be waiting or watching for them And, after Jacob Franks received that call, your Honor, he would have had just sufficient time when he was told to go to that depot, to get on that train going to Michigan City, its final destination Boston

And even then, after receiving the instructions as to what to do in the drug store, he would not know what the ultimate plan was going to be He would have been told, your Honor, had their plans worked out, to go to the rear car of this train and to go to this telegraph blank box, and that there he would find a letter, and to proceed immediately to the rear platform, to open the letter and read it

Then what did the letter state? It told Jacob Franks to turn to the east, and to watch for a large red brick factory with a black water tower on it, and the word " Champion " inscribed on the tower, to have the money ready and as he reached the south end of the factory described in this letter, to count five hurriedly, and then throw it

The Loeb-Leopold Case

They planned to go to the vicinity of this factory, your Honor, where they had been several times prior to that, and be unobserved. They had a place where they could stand, and with the field glasses that they had used for observing the little tots at play, they were to observe this train approaching And if that train should be late, your Honor, or slow down at that particular point, they had it planned to drive on, fearing trouble

Why, it would not be possible to apprehend them in a hundred thousand years Think of the perfection of that plan Not even Jacob Franks, your Honor, knew what was going to happen until he got on that train at 63rd Street, if their plans had worked out, and by the time he had reached 74th Street, he had disposed of the money.

And on Friday morning Leopold went to the University of Chicago, your Honor, and there proceeded to take this entrance examination for Harvard one of the great universities of the world, and his intellect enabled him to safely pass

And while Leopold was taking this examination for Harvard, Loeb said to some newspaper reporters, " Why don't you go along 63rd Street and try and locate those drug stores that they were calling to and from? Let me go along with you I will help you to find them ' Your Honor will remember that Jacob Franks, in his excitement, had forgotten the number of the street to which he had been told to go by Leopold

The Loeb-Leopold Case

And after going, your Honor, to the various places until they reached this particular drug store at 1465 East 63rd Street, upon making inquiry in there, they were informed that on that day of May 22nd two telephone calls had come to that drug store inquiring for Jacob Franks, and after sending that information back to their papers, they started over to the vicinity of the Franks home

And one of the newspaper boys turned to Loeb and asked Loeb if he knew Bobby Franks He said he did, that Bobby Franks used to play tennis in his yard, and said, in reply to a question as to what kind of a fellow he was, that if one was going to pick out a boy to kidnap or murder he was just the kind of a little cocky ——— he would pick

Just imagine that, your Honor, coming from the murderer two days after the boy had been murdered Does not that show an abandoned and malignant heart? Then they decided that they had better dispose of the little class pin, and belt, and shoes of Bobby, so they drove out into Indiana, and hid them out there Then they returned

And while he was talking to Captain Wolff, in answer to the question whether there were any members of his class or any of his friends who wore glasses, Leopold named his companion George Lewis And that night, fearing that by some chance they might pick him out, he stole the typewriter, this Underwood portable typewriter, from his house unnoticed, and placed it in the back of his machine, and Loeb twisted off the keys They threw the typewriter in one lagoon, the keys in another

And then they went home after making up their alibi story and agreeing that if they were called in within a week and questioned they would tell the story, but if they were called in after a week they would not remember where they were on that day

In the meantime, your Honor, we began trying to find out who was the owner of the glasses that had been found at the culvert It was soon learned who were the makers of the frames and that Almer Coe & Co of this city handled the goods of that manufacturer Upon visiting Almer Coe & Co the makers of the frames immediately recognized the frame as their own special design, and they recognized the lenses as their lenses by the peculiar mark on the lens, — and I want to say now, your Honor, if it had not been for the systematic and efficient method Almer Coe & Co use in keeping their records, Nathan Leopold, Jr , and Richard Loeb would be walking the streets today

That stalwart business man, Almer Coe himself, with his manager, Jacob Weinstein, said, " We will place our entire force at work and check back the records and see if we can find a prescription to tally with the glasses "

And they did, and they gave us the names of three people, one a prominent lawyer in this community, another a young lady, and the third Nathan Leopold, Jr., all prescriptions identically the same.

The Loeb-Leopold Case

The lawyer was out of the city, the lady had her glasses on, and then Nathan Leopold, Jr was called in and he told the story previously agreed upon by him and Loeb

"Nathan, have you your glasses at home?" asked the State's Attorney "Yes"

"Do those glasses resemble yours?" And Leopold takes the glasses and examines them and makes the statement, your Honor "If I were not sure my glasses were at home, I would say these are mine"

The State's Attorney requested him to visit his home, accompanied by the police officers, and to find his glasses. When he arrived at his home he looked and looked and looked and went to a drawer where he picked out the case that he had received when he purchased the glasses, and he handed the case to one of the police officers, and said "This is my case, with the name of Almer Coe on the face of it"

But he couldn't find his glasses and the police officers brought Nathan Leopold back to the LaSalle Hotel.

Before Leopold had returned to the hotel Richard Loeb had been brought in, and upon being asked to trace his footsteps — keeping in mind, your Honor, that the week had elapsed the day before, and that the alibi that they had framed was not to be on after a week — Loeb lost his memory and could not say where he was on that particular day

The State's Attorney, leading him step by step, asked him if it was not a fact that on the 21st he had lunch with Leopold at Marshall Field's grill Loeb then knew that Leopold had told the alibi story, and he immediately proceeded to tell his story, the same as Leopold, and convincing every one in that room, your Honor, that he was telling the absolute truth

And after he had gone over his story, which varied in no respect after he started to tell it, the State's Attorney asked him what he thought about the glasses, and Loeb said "Why every one says that if you find the owner of the glasses you have found the man who murdered Bobbie Franks"

The State's Attorney then said to him "Richard, what would you say if I told you that your pal, Nathan Leopold, is the owner of the glasses?" Why, your Honor, he almost jumped out of his seat, and gasped "My God! Why, that can't be true, and if it is true it could not be Nathan that had anything to do with this crime Why, I was with him on that day in question" And the State's Attorney said to him "Yes, Richard, I know you were"

He was taken from the room, and Leopold was brought back and upon being asked if he had found his glasses he stated that he had not, and that these glasses must be his

Then he was asked to explain how it was possible for his glasses to be approximately ten or twelve feet from the culvert where this boy was buried, and he had the most wonderful explanation "Why," he said, " that is nothing, Judge, I have been around that location two hundred times Why, it is only last Saturday I was out there with George Lewis, I was out there with Sidney Stein, and, Judge, on Sunday, I made another visit, I was there again Sunday with Sidney Stein, and it is more than likely that I dropped my glasses from my pocket "

And then he was asked, " Well, Nathan, you stated that you have not worn your glasses for four or five months What were you doing with your glasses in your pocket if you were not wearing them? " And he said that the bird suits, the suits that he used on his ornithology expeditions, were hanging in the closets sometimes two or three months not being pressed, and that in all probability he had left the glasses in one of these suits.

And he remembered in particular on this Sunday that he wanted to shoot some bird and the bird was over, your Honor, in Hyde Lake, and he remembered going across that particular spot, and that he ran from the direction of Wolf Lake toward Hyde Lake, and that he stumbled while he was trying to shoot that bird, and that that must have been the time that he lost his glasses

And then he was asked to put the glasses in his pocket, then he was asked to trip on the floor and he was asked to stumble on the floor, and he tripped and stumbled and he fell and the glasses still remained in his pocket And then he was asked to remove his coat, your Honor, and then he was asked to pick up that coat by the tail, and when he did the glasses fell out of the pocket. That was the way it had actually occurred. Loeb had so handed the coat to Leopold at the culvert.

The defendant Leopold was told that an Underwood typewriter had been recently seen at his home, and he said, if so it must have belonged to one of four boys who had been doing some " dope sheeting " with him. And he named the four boys who had worked with him on his class work and in preparing for an examination in school.

Just about that time Goldstein and Milroy of the *Daily News* came to the State's Attorney's office with some copies of work that had been done on this Underwood portable typewriter.

The boys he referred to were sent for, and upon being questioned in the office, stated that they had noticed at one time in particular this portable typewriter in the home of Nathan Leopold. One of them had made some notes on it.

And after talking to the four boys himself, Leopold was asked the question " Could it be possible that somebody else whose name you have not mentioned owned that typewriter? " His reply was " I think it belongs to Leon Mandel." Leon Mandel was in Europe at that time.

Then he was questioned, and by the questions that were asked of him by the State's Attorney, he was shown that if the typewriter belonged to Leon Mandel, it must still be at his home, and that he agreed

The Loeb-Leopold Case

to He said that he would go out to his home and look for the typewriter, and he did so, accompanied by some of the police officers from the State's Attorney's office

He returned, and upon his return he found that Bernard Hunt, the watchman, who had picked up the bloody chisel on 49th and Greenwood Avenue, was in the office, and he found that Englund, the chauffeur for the family, and his wife were in the office, and he had learned that Englund had told the story that on the particular day in question Leopold's car was in the garage, and that Leopold had requested him to fix the brakes on that car

Leopold and Loeb both now knew that these facts were in possession of the State's Attorney, and Loeb proceeded to tell his story, figuring if he told his story first he might be able to shift the full responsibility upon Leopold

And Leopold, finding out that Loeb was talking, said he would tell the truth about the whole matter and he proceeded to tell his story

And they told it, and after they told it they were both brought into the same room, the king and the slave, and there they sat facing each other while one stenographer read the statement of one to the other, and then in turn back again

Loeb charged the origin of the crime to Leopold, and said that Leopold struck the four blows on the head of Bobbie Franks, Leopold denied it, and asserted that Loeb was the one who killed the boy.

After going into that in detail, they were taken from the State's Attorney's office to make the rounds or to cover the particular spots that they had told about

We first went to the Rent-a-Car people and Leopold was recognized then to the store on Wabash Avenue where Loeb had waited for a telephone call As Loeb was being identified here he fainted

We then proceeded with Leopold to the hardware store where the chisel and rope had been purchased by Loeb The clerk remembered the sale The next stop was at the drug store whose proprietor remembered selling the bottle of hydrochloric acid

Next we went to Leopold's home where the boots and cap were found, then to the bridge from which the typewriter had been dropped and to the other bridge where the detached keys had been thrown, then to the foot of the lake where a robe soaked in blood and partially burned was found, and on to the other places where the class pin, shoes, buckle, etc had been thrown

On the following day, your Honor, they were again returned to the State's Attorney's office where Dr Church, Dr Patrick and Dr Krohn, alienists, and also three chemists, were present, and police officers, and again they told their stories as before

And from there into the jail yard, and while in the jail yard, your Honor, always looking out for themselves, Leopold got into the car, that car that was used when the little boy was murdered, and Loeb refused to get in unless he could get at the wheel, where Leopold was seated He was not going to get into the car, he said, and have them think that he was the one that struck the foul blows

And they returned to the office and as the doctors told your Honor they were examined, and that night they were sent back to the police station And the next day, as your Honor knows, they were taken from the custody of the State's Attorney and turned over to the Sheriff

And after returning from the Coroner's inquest they were brought into the State's Attorney's office and there they were asked if they wanted their suitcases transferred to the jail, and they said they most respectfully declined to answer upon advice of counsel

Does that indicate to your Honor that Leopold and Loeb didn't have the capacity to follow instructions? And they followed them to the letter and refused to talk and that ended it, that ended the State's case; that ended the checking up on every point that they told in their statement but there was not one thing, your Honor, that they had mentioned that was not traced and substantiated

And then the letter from the train that had been placed on there and gone to four or five different cities was forwarded from New York, and as Andy Russo, the electrician in the New Haven yard, told your Honor, he found this letter in the car, in the telegraph blank box and addressed to Jacob Franks

And then the next step was the finding of the typewriter. And that was the last straw.

And then counsel say that they want you to listen to evidence in mitigation, that you have listened to the evidence in aggravation. And they proceed to introduce their evidence, and the first witness, if the court please, that they call, is Dr White from Washington.

He starts off before your Honor, and with all your years of experience I think it would be safe to say that you never before heard two murderers referred to as " Babe " and " Dickie ".

Then he went on to explain to your Honor the reason why he called Leopold " Babe ", because one day he was in the cell talking to " Dickie," and " Babe " told him that unless he would call him " Babe " he wouldn't play any more. So he proceeded to call Leopold " Babe ' and Loeb " Dickie ".

And then he told your Honor that he could tell when they were telling the truth, that he could look into their minds, and that he knew when they were lying.

He then proceeded to tell your Honor about this king-slave phantasy, and about how Leopold looked up to Loeb as the king, and he is the slave, and that all the king had to do was to indicate to the slave what he wanted, and his wish would be carried out, and that the slave was waiting for an opportunity to go to Europe, to get away from this plot, but he was unable to get away from the king, who had him chained with this golden chain

Then he went on and he told your Honor that the boys were mentally diseased — but not quite enough to be insane

And he said he saw a picture, a picture of the boy Richard Loeb in a cowboy's uniform, and that the serious expression on his face signified to him that Loeb had a phantasy, a phantasy to lead a crowd of criminals, a phantasy to be the leader of a gang

And then he told your Honor about his stealing, that he stole articles here and there, and that he burned up shacks

He did not know whether this bonfire, or arson, as he put it, occurred on an election night, or on a Hallowe'en night, or when it occurred But it suited his purpose to say that Loeb had criminalistic tendencies, and that this was a phantasy of his, and that he had had this phantasy from the time he was a little boy

Is there anything unnatural about a little fellow to burn shacks, wagons, fences? To steal? To lie?

And then, your Honor, he speaks of Leopold's philosophy — Leopold's strange philosophy of life, this philosophy that made him a superman, this philosophy that told him so long as he satisfied his own pleasures, it was all right, that he would weigh the amount of pain with the amount of pleasure, and if there was greater pleasure to be derived than there was pain, then he would perform the act.

The Loeb-Leopold Case

And he tells your Honor that that indicated to him, that philosophy, that he was mentally diseased And he tells your Honor that this defendant Leopold would lie down and before he would go to sleep, he would have phantasies

Why, every one has phantasies, and the only difference between the other people, your Honor, and this defendant is that they respect the law of God and man and he respected neither

How many men walking the streets today have evil phantasies, or desires, your Honor? But they pass them out of their minds

But not so with this superman As he argued in the criminal law class at the University of Chicago, he thought that a superman was above the law

Dr Hulbert brings in before your Honor his report, but says, on cross-examination, that the defendants, when being examined, would not go into certain things upon advice of counsel And he told your Honor upon being questioned that if he had received the other information that they refused to divulge, his opinion might have been different

And if his opinion might have been different, your Honor, it is fair to assume that the opinions of the other three doctors who relied on the Bowman-Hulbert report might have been different, too

In conclusion, your Honor has never had a case before you with such evidence presented for mitigation as you have had in this case

Why, your Honor, at the outset of this case, Mr

The Loeb-Leopold Case

Darrow walks in before the court, and makes a virtue out of a necessity He pleads both defendants guilty before your Honor to murder, and to kidnaping for ransom There was no escape

He asks your Honor for mercy, and he tells your Honor that they are both youths, boys What mercy did they give that little tot?

Of course, your Honor, we all feel sorry for the families of these defendants highly respected citizens in this community Your Honor feels sorry for them, and so do I, and you feel sorry for every family, because they are the ones who always suffer, and you feel sorry for the Franks family, and you feel sorry for the mother who still believes that her little boy will yet return

Mr Darrow Where is the evidence on that, Mr. Savage?

Mr Savage· It is a fair inference

Mr Darrow. Oh!

Mr Savage That is fair to infer, your Honor, that that mother who cherished the boy is still waiting for his return from school, and then they ask your Honor for mercy!

Why, your Honor, the law is made for all people, rich and poor, Jew or Gentile, black or white

And these two murderers sitting before your Honor are not immune to that law Justice sits by, and the world looks on, and this community, the community, your Honor, where every mother and father should get down on their knees and give to

Almighty God their thanks that their daughter was not the victim of this fiendish conspiracy, as Leopold planned

Why Judge, if ever there was a case in history that deserves the most severe punishment, this is the case And I want to say, your Honor, that if your Honor does not hang both of these murderers, it will be a long time in Cook County before we ever hang another Capital punishment will mean nothing in our law and might as well be abolished.

And I want to say to your Honor that the men who have reached the gallows prior to this time have been unjustly treated, if these two do not follow I know your Honor will live up to his full responsibility, and that you will enforce the law as you see it should be enforced The people of this great community are looking to your Honor to mete out justice, that justice that the murderers in this case so richly deserve

And when your Honor metes out that justice we will have no more supermen, we will have no more men with phantasies, whose desires are to ravish young children and then murder them

And, your Honor, when you inflict the extreme penalty in this case, you will have told the world that Cook County is a safe place for one's children, and that the people will have no fear for their children's lives when they are returning home from school

And you will have set, your Honor, that confidence in our laws and in our justice that will waver if we fail to see that the defendants here are properly punished

You will so stabilize the administration of the law here that all will realize that it applies to them no matter what their station in life may be

And without going into it, your Honor, your Honor well knows what juries have said in your court room, and in other court rooms since your Honor has been the Chief Justice of this court, that murder must stop, and the only way you will stop murder is by hanging the murderers, and if your Honor hangs these two murderers, it will set an example to the others, if we have any of them among us, that justice is swift, and that justice is sure, and that if they fail to live up to the law they will receive its sure and certain penalty

Speech of Walter Bachrach

IF YOUR HONOR PLEASE, GENTLEMEN

THE position of the defense in this case has been much distorted in the arguments of the State's Attorneys who have preceded me, as well as in the daily press, and therefore it is my desire at the outset to make clear our position with regard to the subject of mental disease in this case

We raise no issue as to the legal sanity of these defendants and make no contention that by reason of the fact that they are suffering from a diseased mental condition, there should be any division or lessening of the responsibility to answer for the crime, the commission of which they have confessed We do assert that they are suffering and were suffering at the time of the commission of the crime charged from a diseased mental condition, but we do not concern ourselves with the question of whether such mental disease would constitute in the present case a defense to the charge of murder By the pleas of guilty the defendants have assumed complete responsibility for the crime of murder, and this is in nowise a proceeding in which an effort is being made to lessen that responsibility

The subject matter of this proceeding is the assessment of punishment for the crime committed and such assessment is placed by our law within the discretion of your Honor Our statute provides that the crime of murder shall be punishable by a sentence of imprisonment in the penitentiary for a period of not less than fourteen years, or for life, or by death Where there has been a plea of guilty to such crime, as in this case, the statute provides, " It shall be the duty of the court to hear witnesses in aggravation and mitigation of the offense "

The crime has been judicially confessed by the pleas of guilty Complete criminal responsibility has been assumed by the defendants, and your Honor is now in this proceeding hearing witnesses in aggravation and mitigation of the offense as a basis for the assessment of the punishment

It is as though there were before your Honor a sort of sliding scale with imprisonment in the penitentiary for fourteen years at one end and punishment by death at the other, and as though it were your Honor's duty to set the indicator at some point upon this scale. The whole subject matter being discussed here and upon which the evidence is being introduced and the witnesses heard, relates directly and solely to the question at what point upon that sliding scale your Honor should fix the indicator and thereby determine the punishment to be imposed upon the defendants for the crime to which they have pleaded guilty

It is our position that the defendants are suffering and were suffering at the time of the commission of the crimes with which they are charged from a diseased condition of the mind, and that such diseased mental condition of each defendant is a circumstance which should be considered by this court in the determination of the proper sentence to be imposed upon them

The consequences — the objective anti-social consequences — of murder are precisely the same in every case. In a case where a victim is struck upon the head four times, the anti-social consequences of that murder are just the same as if that person had been struck but once. If the act is done with malice, so far as society is concerned, it is murder.

But your Honor may hear evidence in mitigation. To do this it is necessary to pass upon the offender. Let me illustrate. A man who believes his wife has been seduced by another, kills that other man. The anti-social consequences of that act are the same as if he had had no such belief in his mind at the time of the killing. The other man has been killed, and the shooting was done with malice.

But, under the statute, in fixing the punishment, your Honor looks to see if there was anything lessening the turpitude of the offender. Was there something in his reaction to a given situation which creates a circumstance which the court ought to consider in mitigation of the punishment?

There are many persons who walk the streets who are subject to mental disease falling short of the legal definition of insanity, and when one of these persons commits a homicide and admits the crime, the question as to whether or not there is any mitigation requires an assessment of the circumstances pertaining to the character of the offender.

Now there is an analogy if your Honor please, between mental disease and youth. Youth in a criminal is a mitigating circumstance. Youth involves a question of stress and strain of puberty and adolescence. Your Honor will recall some of the evidence in this case to the effect that a child is born without morals, and as a result of education, teaching by others, he in time acquires a sense of moral values.

A person with mental disease likewise has a lack of fixed social habits. Mental disease is primarily the inability on the part of the person suffering to make a successful adjustment to the environment in which he lives and, therefore, a person suffering from a mental disease is in relatively the same position as a child who has not been able, by reason of lack of time, lack of experience, lack of opportunity, to form fixed social habits, and make proper adjustments to a complex world.

In view of these facts it has been judicially recognized by the Supreme Court of Nebraska in *Tracy vs The State, 64 N W, 1069,* that youth, diseased mental condition, and numerous other factors of a similar character, should be taken into consideration by the court in fixing the punishment.

Your Honor has ruled that such evidence is admissible on the question of mitigation of punishment, and I take it, in view of that ruling, and in view of that case, which is the only case squarely passing upon the question, we have a right to assume that if the defense has established mental disease in this case, the defendants are entitled to have your Honor consider it as a mitigating circumstance here.

The State's Attorneys have laid much stress upon the proposition that your Honor ought to follow the law and an attempt has been made to give the impression that there is some sort of a legal precedent somewhere which requires your Honor to impose a death penalty in this case. There is no such law.

Your Honor has been given the discretion, in cases where pleas of guilty are entered, to fix a penalty anywhere between a minimum and a maximum term of years, or at death.

Your Honor stands in the relationship of a father to these defendants. Every judge does. Every man in his heart knows that the judge on the bench is his father, his punisher, when he is wrong, that he must come before him and receive his chastisement. But when he comes before his legal father on a plea of guilty, that father is faced with the duty which every father has of desiring understanding of the wrongdoer, and what it was that brought about the situation, before the punishment is inflicted. It is so easy to hang, the important problem is put out of sight. It requires more intelligence to investigate.

Your Honor, don't the very circumstances of this crime, the details of which we have heard recited here a number of times — recited with emphasis, with adverbs and adjectives — don't these circumstances show abnormal mental condition?

Let us start, if your Honor please, with the first of June. By that time the confessions of the boys were in and had been fully corroborated. And the first thing the State's Attorney did, if your Honor please, was to have what Mr Darrow designated as a " roundup." He sent out his call for his alienists

The Loeb-Leopold Case

Why should the idea of insanity ever have entered Mr Crowe's mind? The answer is quite clear in the testimony of one of his own experts, Dr Patrick, when he was asked his opinion upon his observations made of these defendants on the first of June in the State's Attorney's office He said "With the exception of the facts surrounding this crime, excluding those facts, in my opinion there is not any evidence to show that the boys were mentally diseased on the 21st of May, 1924"

Excluding those facts! Now, why did he exclude them?

Because those facts were of such a peculiar character that the first suggestion that would come into anybody's mind would be that it was the act of the insane or mentally diseased

Suppose that some one were to come to your Honor, or to anybody who knows my associate, Mr Darrow, who has known him for years, and knows the kindly individual that he is, and say that Mr Darrow had kidnaped and murdered a boy fourteen years old, and brought you proof that he had done it Would your Honor say that Mr Darrow was a hardened murderer, or would you not rather suggest that his mind had become affected?

Now, that was the situation, if your Honor please, that was presented to Robert Crowe These were respected boys, intelligent, without the earmarks of criminals, the sons of respected parents of wealth and stability When they had confessed the crime, what happened was the very natural thing that would happen in a situation like that, namely, that Mr Crowe would doubt their sanity, and doubting their sanity, he sent for Dr Patrick, Dr Church and Dr. Krohn, who came on Sunday

They went through what I regard as a farcical performance, and not alone farcical, but there was something terrible about it Here is a proceeding being conducted in the office of the State's Attorney of Cook County, at which there are present anywhere from fifteen people up Dr Patrick comes into the room, and carries on a little conversation with Nathan Leopold, Jr , about birds, about ornithology A little later Dr Krohn comes in and they have a little conversation about psychology, about various tests out at the university

Then they go down in the jail yard, and see the automobile But before that, Loeb tells the story of this crime There are a few interruptions, and comments back and forth by Nathan Leopold, Jr , and Loeb, and arguments between them as to which one struck the fatal blow Then the State's alienists leave, and they are ready upon such observations to come into court and give testimony, the effect of which may send two human beings to the gallows

These alienists, if your Honor please, testified that these boys are not mentally diseased, because they did not show evidence of mental disease

Their evidence is based entirely upon negative findings Now, it is a well known principle of logic that you cannot prove a positive by a negative. Ten thousand facts showing the absence of mental disease would be as easily toppled over as one fact by the proof of the presence of a single fact demonstrating such disease.

Unless the alienists for the State examined these boys along the very lines and upon the very points that the alienists for the defense did, then the evidence of the alienists for the State along these lines and on these points is without value.

To suppose that people are well mentally because they are oriented to time, space and persons, because they know who they are and where they are, recognize people about them, show good memory, are logical and coherent in their responses to questions asked, is just as naïve as to suppose that a person is well mentally because he is not a raving maniac.

Your Honor will recall that Dr. Patrick testified on cross-examination that he had never before conducted an examination as to mental condition under such circumstances. Dr. Church had never conducted any such examination under similar conditions. The only alienist for the State who stated that the conditions under which the examination was made were favorable was Dr. William O. Krohn, and his conclusions as to the mental condition of the defendants in this case on the 21st of May, 1924, were based upon what he called the memory, which he said was intact, the capacity of logical reasoning, and orientation.

The Loeb-Leopold Case

I wish to read an extract here from " The Recognition of Insanity " by Eugen Bleuler, director of the psychiatric clinic at Vienna

One must never conclude that if there is no affective disturbance, that therefore it is not a case of schizophrenia Indeed, under certain circumstances, even in a pronounced psychosis or mental disease, one can temporarily find nothing morbid A negative finding without prolonged observation, therefore never proves that the patient is normal It only indicates an absence of proof of the disease

Now, your Honor, when the defendants were examined by the defense alienists could the boys have been malingering? Doctors Singer and Krohn, State witnesses, in their book, " Insanity and the Law," say

Since simulation is not a disease, it cannot be said that there are any characteristic symptoms The most practical way to deal with the problem, therefore, seems to be to consider the points that may be of assistance in distinguishing each of the major types of reaction It may be pointed out in general that though insanity is evidenced chiefly by subjective signs, that is to say, by signs that are within the individual's control, the simulation of insanity requires a knowledge of the various types of insanity, and also a capacity for self-control that is possessed by very few The effort must be continued day and night under all conditions Unexpected and unforeseen circumstances must continually arise that will distract the attention from the purpose of deception, and will betray to the attentive observer the fact that the complaints are not genuine Few laymen and indeed few physicians possess sufficient knowledge of the symptoms of insanity to know how to act in accordance with any particular form of insanity. Even if a man does possess this information it would be necessary for him to think before responding to any situation, and the facts of lack of spontaneity and the need for a choice of response will almost certainly give rise to incongruities which cannot fail to excite suspicion if the observer is on the watch for them

I quote the following from page 1259 of the transcript of evidence, Dr White on the stand

Q In making an examination of a patient, what are your criteria of dependability and veracity with respect to what the patient tells you? In other words, can you tell when the patient is lying and when he is telling the truth?

A The criteria are the inherent quality of the evidence presented and its coherence with known laws of the operation of the mind. If evidence given by a patient departs from well known laws of mental operation, we have the right to question the veracity of the patient. If it is consistent with those well known laws, we have a right to assume, at least for the time being, that a patient is telling the truth. Now, with regard to a specific statement, one's judgment might not be conclusive, but if after talking for hours and hours and getting a description from the patient of all sorts of mental states and attitudes of mind, and historical factors, we find that the picture presents a coherent whole, that it unfolds itself in accordance with the known laws of the operation of the mind, then we know that that picture is substantially true

In a brief interview, it might be possible for a normal person to dissemble in some minor respects and create a suspicion that he might be mentally diseased. But such dissembling is impossible where the examination is conducted under conditions such as existed when the examinations were made by the defense experts, examinations covering a long period of time, not made by one expert alone, but made by four, and where the four experts arrive at a common understanding as to what the facts are — five experts, because Dr. Bowman also examined these boys, and, although he did not testify, his report is in evidence. The book of Doctors Singer and Krohn corroborates the evidence of Doctor White.

So that you have the verity in the different examinations as to facts arrived at by five experts covering a long period of time in the case of the defense's examination as against the examination made by the State's experts in the instance of Drs. Patrick, Church and Krohn late one afternoon, and by Dr. Singer the next day, after the boys had been turned over to the sheriff and taken from the custody of the State's Attorney by means of a habeas corpus writ, and when they were brought into Mr. Crowe's office and declined to answer any questions about anything because they had been told by their lawyers not to answer questions.

The impression is sought to be created that because these boys were able to repeat parrotlike in answer to the questions asked by Drs. Krohn and Singer, that they respectfully refused to answer, upon advice of counsel, therefore, there was no evidence of mental disease The absurdity of such a position is apparent

In the first place, if your Honor please, these boys are not claimed by the defense to be stupid There is no claim made that they do not know how to reason, nor that they have not good memory There is no claim made that they don't know where they are They know things occur, they know they are being tried on a plea of guilty as to the question of punishment They have intelligence

The evidence is that because of their superior intellects, because they progressed at an unusually great rate of speed, and on account of the slow development of their emotional life, a split in the personality of these boys has occurred

That is, as respects Nathan Leopold, Jr , we have an individual whose powers of reasoning are intact, which is one of the peculiarities of a paranoid personality

A paranoid personality, to begin with, must be a person of superior intellect He must be a person who is capable of reasoning well The only trouble with his logic is he starts with the wrong premise, and that is what makes him a paranoiac Usually he has delusions of grandeur, he has delusions that he is greater than anybody else. He identifies himself with some great religious character, with some king, or with some potentate, or with Christ, or with God And as far back as October, 1923, Leopold was talking about the superman

And let me digress for a moment merely to say that there is no claim made here that the fact Leopold believes he is a superman entitles him to any consideration for his philosophy We are not here to defend his philosophy

What we claim is, if the court please, that the belief shows he is mentally diseased, that his mind is not functioning properly, that he has the tendencies of what is called a paranoid personality

I call your Honor's attention to the letter dated October 10, 1923, written by Nathan Leopold, Jr, to his co-defendant, Richard Loeb *

Here is a letter, if your Honor please, in which a superman in his own estimation — which is significant not because he is but because he thinks he is — lays down the code to be obeyed by his companion, Richard Loeb, whom he generously also allows to go under the designation of superman, but for whom he, Leopold, establishes a code of conduct

In addition to the evidence contained in this letter you have the testimony of the various fellow students of Leopold at the University of Chicago, who testified to conversations with him in which he stated his conception of the superman his philosophy of Hedonism, his individualistic philosophy, the fact that he had a right to do anything if it pleased him

The fact that he felt that he could live out such

---

* EDITOR'S NOTE — The letter here referred to by Mr Bachrach is printed in full beginning on page 222 of this volume

a philosophy in a complicated world like this, and the fact that he was to be the judge, the sole judge, as to whether a thing was right, if it gave him pleasure, is evidence bearing upon the question as to whether his is a paranoid personality

In Messrs Singer and Krohn's book again under the head of "Paranoid Psychoses," the authors say

Assuming, then, the typical state of well developed energy of reaction, the paranoid personality may be described more concretely as follows The man is a dominant, aggressive person, anxious to be in the forefront and careless of the feelings and interests of others He takes life seriously, works hard and with purpose

Just as Leopold did He worked with his birds, he was a teacher of ornithology, all the things he did required seriousness of purpose and hard work

He is always sure of himself, is satisfied with his own views and constantly endeavors to impose them on others He is quick to take affront, yet seldom fights openly, and continually seeks for hidden motives and meanings behind the words and acts of others that do not tend to his own advantage or accord with his own views

Leopold's letter to Loeb clearly indicates all of this

The authors also say

The increased feelings of interference with securing personal satisfaction lead to close observation of the sayings and doings of others, with the object of detecting plots and schemes that are responsible for his own failures

Note the close observation here, if your Honor please, as shown by the letter of Leopold to Loeb of

The Loeb-Leopold Case

October 10, 1923, of the sayings and doings of his friend Richard Loeb. Note the close observation of the fact that Loeb made a mistake as to who was the founder of Stoicism and that that constitutes to Leopold a greater crime even than murder.

Also, on page 74:

> Throughout, the intelligence remains intact; perception is clear and there is no disorientation in the narrower sense of this term. Memory is good, in spite of the falsifications in meaning and context that have been mentioned. The man remains in contact with reality, active, alert and interested and there is no tendency to deterioration or dementia. Hallucinations are unusual, though they may occur during periods of marked excitement.

Dr. Krohn testified that he based his judgment as to the absence of mental disease of Leopold, upon his memory, his logical processes, and his orientation, and his senses: but these are all shown by his own book to be no evidence that a mental disease did not exist, but are entirely compatible with the existence of a paranoid psychosis.

Now, let us see what they have to say about Loeb.

On page 53, in discussing schizophrenic psychosis, or dementia praecox, appears this statement:

> Schizophrenia, literally translated, means splitting of the mind. It is not possible to look inside of the mind, hence, conclusions concerning its operation are based on observation of what the person says and does, these

The Loeb-Leopold Case

being the resultants of his mental activity In this category must be included the activities of the involuntary muscles and glands, which cooperate in every activity of the body, and play an especially prominent rôle in such as are accompanied by emotion

Then it is further said here

The intelligence of schizophrenic persons is usually good and is often above the average Indeed, it seems probable that high grade intelligence is necessary for the development of this mode of reaction In certain respects, the reactions are exaggerations or caricatures of the modification of primitive instinctive adjustments that make social existence possible and that is brought about by the evolution of symbolic thinking

The facts are usually far better explained by recognizing that there has been a failure to establish memories or associations (intellectual deficiency) as a result of the unusually early and extensive development of a tendency to autism which we shall discuss shortly Typically, perception and the formation of memories with clear grasp and orientation are fully up to the average The trouble lies not in the quality of the intellectual tools, but in the use that is made of them

Again you have a statement in Singer and Krohn's own book that the fact that judgment was possessed, orientation was possessed, memory was possessed, is no indication that in Loeb there are not the schizophrenic tendencies developing into a psychosis

I continue reading from this volume, published at a very appropriate time

The Loeb-Leopold Case

We have described the essence of the schizophrenic reaction as a bashful timidity associated with lack of energy. Consequently, the situations that will render it manifest are such as require self-assertion and active participation in the world of reality. So long as the individual can keep within himself and avoid the necessity for rubbing shoulders with his fellows, he may show but little evidence of difficulty. But it must be remembered that even with himself, there are desires struggling for expression and gratification toward which he may be just as timid as he is toward other persons. Obviously, the period of life during which, as a rule, the demands for adjustment will be least is that of childhood. Then, responsibilities are few and instinctive desires are relatively simple and but little subject to social regulation. The sexual and parental instincts are as yet only foreshadowed and it is in this sphere especially that society places the greatest restrictions on individual behavior.

The schizophrenic child is quiet and retiring, prefers solitary games and amusements, and lacks the aggressive spontaneity and outspoken sensuality of the average child. He does not get into mischief and is often described as " unusually good," " never caused a moment's trouble,' docile and easily amused. He may be fairly even tempered and yet subject to rather violent and perhaps unexpected outbursts of emotion on seemingly small occasion, usually short-lived. He is affectionate though undemonstrative and displays his feelings little. He makes few friends and no confidants, in group games he is often on the outside looking in, rather than an active participant. This is not due, necessarily, to an ineptitude for athletic activities — he may even excel in them — but to the difficulty in getting outside himself.

In school he often does extremely well so far as scholastic acquisitions are concerned He is liable to be absorbed in books —

All of which applies literally to Richard Loeb —

Mr Crowe Mr Bachrach the statement "All of which applies literally to Richard Loeb," is not in the book, is it?

Mr Bachrach No The book was written before this case arose I continue reading

He is liable to be absorbed in books and especially in topics that are philosophic and abstract rather than those that would bring him into dealing with the real and the concrete Often the school successes give rise to hopes of a brilliant future, incapable of realization because of the impossibility of effectively meeting reality

As the stronger passions and feelings develop, the difficulties in expressing them become proportionately greater and there is an increasing tendency for the youth to shut himself up within himself (autism) and to dream rather than to react openly The process of repression and substitution results in the appearance of mannerisms and oddities in behavior, often with increased bashfulness and awkward clumsiness, when the schizophrenic is obliged to mix with others or when his desires and feelings are touched on

Oftentimes, these persons develop wonderful dreams of the futures for which they are destined, but these remain as veritable 'castles in Spain, unpractical and without the application that would be necessary to bring them to fruition

The dreams and plans are vague and indefinite, though possibly highly colored, and little consideration is given to the practical facts of the situation The mood is often exalted, but instead of leading to increased activity and sensual interest, it takes the form rather of an ecstatic dreaming On the other hand, the mood may be of depressive color and is then evidenced by fretful worrying, with irritability, and is ineffective in producing any change in the situation

Sometimes it is rather a moody brooding with occasional outbursts of violence

It would be a mistake to assume that every person with a schizophrenic trend is going to develop a psychosis or become insane Very many never do so at all, possibly because the complexes that are split off do not involve a very large part of the man's personality, or because the conditions under which he has to live do not make demands that he cannot meet sufficiently well to 'get by' One of the subgroups of dementia praecox comprises such individuals under the name of dementia simplex They do not often come under the observation of the psychiatrist and have had little importance for the medical jurist It is readily intelligible however, that the outbreak of a psychosis is especially liable to occur when special demands in the way of responsibility and direct contact with the real world are made One such period is that of leaving school and emancipation from home control another is concerned with the problems of puberty, marriage and the establishment of a home

In this connection let me call your Honor's attention to the evidence that until he was fourteen years of age, Richard Loeb had been completely under the control and domination of a governess At fourteen she ceased to be his governess, and at that time he entered college

It was a time when he had reached puberty and

was approaching adolescence. It was a time when he was taken from that home shelter, from the shelter of this governess and from her domination and control, from the woman who up to that time had solved all of his problems with the world.

That was gone, and he suddenly was put in an environment, a fourteen-year-old boy in college, associated with boys of eighteen, nineteen, twenty and twenty-one, facing the necessity for meeting life as these boys and young men were meeting life, and thereby being put in a position where excessive demands for adjustment to life would be suddenly placed on him. He already had started in as a child, as a schizophrenic personality, whose tendency toward schizophrenia had been cultured and fostered by the particular type of care and attention and lack of understanding which he had received from his governess. I continue the reading:

We would again emphasize the fact that we are not here describing dementia praecox, but only a reaction type. There will, therefore, be no subdivision into the types of that disease. It will, however, be necessary to speak of the deterioration so-called, that seems to be the logical outcome of the psychosis.

First, it should be said that the intellectual mechanism remains undamaged, though this is not always easy of demonstration because the patient is more or less inaccessible to study and examination. The difficulty is increased by the fact that absorption in the dream world, which we find characteristic of the schizophrenic personality, is here exaggerated to such a degree that the real world may be entirely ignored and the man may fail to use his powers of perception and grasp. In consequence, he establishes only scanty and haphazard memories of what transpires around him and may thus seem to have lost his memory.

Now, the evidence here with respect to Richard Loeb is that he started in as a child to have a peculiar type of phantasy. He had a phantasy of being in jail, of being looked at by women through the bars, that he was in a jail yard with women and men who were naked, and he felt ashamed.

We have therefore, in him a peculiar type of phantasy, which is different from the normal phantasies that everybody has, and which have a very definite function, they cause the development of ambition, they cause the development of all those things which will carry the individual forward.

Ordinarily, normal phantasies will do that. But a phantasy to be normal must be one that has a definite relation to the environment of the individual. In other words, a small child has phantasies of being a policeman, of being a fireman, or of being whatever his father is.

If it is a girl, she phantasies the type of person her mother is. She phantasies herself as being a wonderful person. She has all sorts of phantasies which are noble in character and which tend to the development, to the maintaining of life, so to speak, and to the enlargement of the individual.

They are also compensatory. As the individual

becomes older, as time goes on, he finds that some of the things he phantasied about as a child, things that he wanted to have, what he wished to be, are incapable of fulfillment And he, therefore, uses his phantasy life to satisfy this craving, these unsatisfied wishes which he has, and he lives out in his phantasy the kind of a life which is denied to him in this world Those things, of course, are normal

In the case of Richard Loeb, we find he starts in as a child of four and a half or five years of age and has abnormal phantasies, which have not changed as his position in life has changed, and as he has become older, but these abnormal phantasies have continued until he is in jail at the age of nineteen, charged with a kidnaping and murder And he has the same abnormal phantasies even now in jail

Were Singer Krohn and Patrick looking for anything like that? Of course, they were not Their position was "Prima facie you are sane Prima facie you are mentally healthy We must be shown" Therefore, they took the position that if evidence was not produced before them on one afternoon, on the first of June, that the boys were mentally diseased, then there was a conclusive presumption to be drawn against the presence of such disease

On page 765 of the Ninth Edition of Church and Peterson on Nervous and Mental Diseases, appears the following

The Loeb-Leopold Case

The examination of a patient with mental disorder is a much more complex process than that of a physical disorder, for it is necessary in the former not only to ascertain the present physical condition as with ordinary patients, but also to investigate the mental state, which involves the employment of unusual and new methods, and brings us into contact with a novel series of psychic phenomena, and moreover, to attain our end we need to study the whole past life of the patient, his diseases, his accidents, schooling, occupation, environment and character

Nor can we stop here, for it is of the greatest importance to inform ourselves as to conditions among his antecedents to determine the type of family from which he sprang and the presence or absence of an hereditary taint There is therefore much to learn even before seeing the patient in person

Did Patrick did Church, did Singer did Krohn do any of that? Why, they said they never saw the boys before their examinations and never made any investigations about them

I quote from page 774 of this same volume

It was Schopenhauer who said that insanity is a long dream and a dream brief insanity There is in fact more than a superficial resemblance between dreams and insanity, so much so that psychiatrists the world over are devoting themselves to the study of dreams as a part of their clinical and psychiatric work

There is practically no phenomenon that presents itself in dreams that may not be observed among the inmates of any asylum ward

Mr Crowe Pardon me Mr Bachrach There is no evidence here of any dreams.

The Loeb-Leopold Case

Mr Bachrach There is evidence of daydreams

Mr Crowe Well, you are not reading about daydreams now, are you?

Mr Bachrach The same thing

Mr Crowe Are they?

Mr Bachrach Daydreams as well as night dreams, if your Honor please, indicate an undirected functioning of the mind. They, therefore, are not subject to the conscious guidance of the individual, and when the psychiatrist has submitted to him the dreams, night dreams or daydreams, of his patient, he has material that is spontaneous, uncontrolled material, and, therefore, material which forms a basis for a more correct conclusion than merely a controlled history given by the patient

Mr Crowe Will you pardon me, just another question?

Mr Bachrach: Yes

Mr Crowe All this you have been reading about deals with insanity, does it not?

Mr Bachrach: Yes

Mr. Crowe. Is that your defense?

Mr Bachrach It is not. The textbook which I have read deals with nervous and mental diseases, and under the subject of insanity, as used by those gentlemen as indicating a mental disease, and not a legal insanity, they discuss these various symptoms

We do not use the word insanity, if your Honor please, in this case, for the simple reason that we are not dealing with the question of a legal defense at all. Dr. White in his book says:

> Insanity should not be used as a medical term at all. It is solely a legal and sociological concept, and so used to designate those members of the community who are so far from able to adjust themselves to the ordinary social requirements that the community segregates them, forcibly perhaps, and takes away their rights as citizens. Insanity is a form of social inadequacy, which medically may be the result of many varieties of mental disease.

Messrs. Church, Patrick and Krohn failed to comply with any of the conditions laid down in Dr. Church's book for the making of a psychiatric examination. They stopped when they found no proof of disease. They did not look for any disease, although they were put on notice of its possible existence by the circumstances of the crime.

Just take the other side of that picture. The same facts, if your Honor please, as regards this crime served notice on counsel for the defense of the same question, namely, the presence of mental disease, that they served upon the State's Attorney. And the defense arranged with a number of able and distinguished men to make an examination of these boys, with a view of ascertaining their mental condition and reporting that mental condition to us.

They had the facilities offered in the jail in the form of a private cell, large enough for the purpose of their examinations, where they had privacy, and were away from noises and disturbances, and from large crowds, and where they were given the opportunity to make a thorough examination

Now, your Honor will recall that when Dr Krohn was cross-examined by us as to whether there was anything besides what was said by these boys that was taken into consideration, he said yes, the reactions, how they behaved — that that was important

Of how much greater value is the evidence of what the physicians for the defense have done Here, you have a situation where a long period of time was taken, where there were repeated examinations made, and under various conditions, by the experts for the defense And they say these boys are mentally diseased

Bowman and Hulbert, the evidence shows, took fourteen days to gather these facts, and the State's alienists got enough in forty minutes to say that there was not any evidence of mental disease How can the testimony of these witnesses be mentioned in the same breath with that of ours?

To summarize, by way of conclusion of this part of the argument on behalf of the defense upon a plea of guilty to the crime of murder, the statute places upon the court the duty of hearing witnesses in mitigation of the offense

We submit that this means that the court, in fixing the sentence, must take into consideration the circumstances in connection with the offender in the particular case. If those circumstances lessen the turpitude of the offender, it is unquestionably the intent of the Legislature that the court be influenced by such considerations in assessing the punishment.

We further submit, that a diseased mental condition in the offender, retarding his social adjustments and making all the more difficult the problems and conflicts presented during adolescence, is such a mitigating circumstance within the meaning and intent of the statute. Moreover, the evidence demonstrates the existence in Nathan Leopold, Jr. of a paranoid personality, and in Richard Loeb of a schizophrenic condition of mind, which in each boy resulted in diseased mental reactions and made possible the perpetration, in combination, of the crimes committed.

We say that it is not the intent of the law in such a case that the penalty of death shall be paid by the offender, but that in the light of such mitigating circumstances, the court, by the exercise of a wise and humane discretion, should assess punishment at some point in the field of choice short of death, the **extreme penalty of the law.**

The Loeb-Leopold Case

Speech of Clarence Darrow

YOUR HONOR

IT has been almost three months since the great responsibility of this case was assumed by my associates and myself. I am willing to confess that it has been three months of great anxiety, a burden which I gladly would have been spared excepting for my feelings of affection toward some of the members of one of these troubled families.

Our anxiety has not been due to the facts that are connected with this most unfortunate affair, but to the almost unheard of publicity it has received, to the fact that newspapers all over this country have been giving it space such as they have almost never before given to any case.

Almost every person has formed an opinion. And when the public is interested and demands a punishment, it thinks of only one punishment, and that is death. It may not be a question that involves the taking of human life, it may be a question of pure prejudice alone, but when the public speaks as one man it thinks only of killing.

We have been in this stress and strain for three months. We did what we could to gain the confidence of the public, who in the end really control, whether wisely or unwisely.

It was announced that there were millions of dollars to be spent on this case. Wild and extravagant

The Loeb-Leopold Case

stories were freely published as though they were facts. Here was to be an effort to save the lives of two boys by the use of money in fabulous amounts. We announced to the public that no excessive use of money would be made in this case in any way. We have faithfully kept that promise. The psychiatrists, as has been shown by the evidence, are receiving only a per diem, which is the same as is paid by the State. The attorneys, at their own request, have agreed to take such amount as the officers of the Chicago Bar Association may think is proper.

If we fail in this defense it will not be for lack of money. It will be on account of money. Money has been the most serious handicap that we have met. There are times when poverty is fortunate. I insist, your Honor, had this been the case of two boys of these defendants' age, unconnected with families supposed to have great wealth, there is not a State's Attorney in Illinois who would not have consented at once to a plea of guilty and a punishment in the penitentiary for life. No lawyer could have justified any other attitude. We could have come into this court without evidence, without argument, and this court would have given to us what every judge has given to every boy in Chicago since the first capital case was tried.

Lawyers stand here by the day and read cases from the Dark Ages, where judges have said that if a man had a grain of sense left, and a child if he was barely out of his cradle, could be hanged be-

The Loeb-Leopold Case

cause he knew the difference between right and wrong. Death sentences for as low as fourteen years have been cited. I have heard in the last six weeks nothing but the cry for blood. I have heard from the office of the State's Attorney only ugly hate. I have seen a court urged almost to the point of threats to hang two boys in the face of science, in the face of philosophy, in the face of humanity, in the face of experience, and all the better and more humane thought of the age.

My friend, Mr. Marshall, who dug up from the relics of the buried past these precedents that would bring a blush of shame to the face of a savage, could also have read this from his beloved Blackstone that, under fourteen, though an infant should be judged to be incapable of guile prima facie, yet if it appeared to the court and the jury that he was capable of guile, and could discern between good and evil, he might be convicted and suffer death.

Thus a girl thirteen, has been burned for killing her mistress. One boy of ten, and another of nine years of age, who had killed his companion, were sentenced to death, and he of ten actually hanged. Why? He knew the difference between right and wrong. He had learned that in Sunday school.

Why, Mr. Savage says age makes no difference, and that if this court should do what every other court in Illinois has done since its foundation, and refuse to sentence these boys to death, no one else would ever be hanged in Illinois. Well, I can

The Loeb-Leopold Case

imagine some results worse than that. So long as this terrible tool is to be used for a plaything, without thought or consideration, we ought to get rid of it for the protection of human life

Mr. Savage — did you pick him for his name or his ability or his learning? — in as cruel a speech as he knew how to make, said to this court that we plead guilty because we were afraid to do anything else Well, it certainly was not done to help the State I hope we have made no mistake

We did plead guilty before your Honor because we were afraid to submit our cause to a jury I would not for a moment deny to this court or to this community a realization of the serious danger we were in and how perplexed we were before we took this step But I have found that experience with life tempers one's emotions and makes him more understanding of his fellow man When my friend Savage is my age, or even yours, he will read his address to this court with horror

I am aware that as one grows older he is less critical He is not so sure He is inclined to make some allowance for his fellow man I am aware that a court has more experience, more judgment and more kindliness than a jury

I know perfectly well that where responsibility is divided by twelve, it is easy to say "Away with him" But, your Honor, if these boys hang, you must do it. You can never explain that the rest overpowered you It must be by your own deliberate, cool, premeditated act. It was not a kindness to you. We placed this responsibility on your shoulders because we were mindful of the rights of our clients, and we were mindful of the unhappy families who have done no wrong.

Now, let us see, your Honor, what we had to sustain us. Of course, I have known your Honor for a good many years. Not intimately. I could not say that I could even guess from my experience what your Honor might do, but I did know something. I knew, your Honor, that ninety unfortunate human beings had been hanged by the neck until dead in the city of Chicago in our history. We would not have civilization except for those ninety that were hanged, and if we cannot make it ninety-two we will have to shut up shop. Some ninety human beings have been hanged in the history of Chicago, and of those only four have been hanged on the plea of guilty.

I knew that in the last ten years three hundred and forty people have been indicted for murder in the city of Chicago and have pleaded guilty and only one has been hanged! And my friend who is prosecuting this case deserves the honor of that hanging while he was on the bench. But his victim was forty years old.

Yes, we are asking this court to save these lives, which is the least and the most that a judge can do.

The State's Attorneys invoke the dark and cruel past. They say that neither tender years nor condition of mind can mitigate. I can sum up their argument in a minute. *cruel; dastardly, premeditated, fiendish, abandoned and malignant heart —* sounds like a cancer — *cowardly, cold-blooded!*

Now, that is what we have been listening to against two minors, two children, who have no right to sign a note or make a deed.

Cowardly? Well, I don't know. Let me tell you something that I think is cowardly whether their acts were or not. Here is Dickie Loeb and Nathan Leopold and the State objects to anybody calling one "Dickie" and the other "Babe" although everybody does, but they think they can hang them easier if their names are Richard and Nathan. Eighteen and nineteen years old at the time of the homicide. Here are three officers watching them. Not a chance to get away. Handcuffed when they get out of this room. Not a chance. Penned like rats in a trap, and for a lawyer with physiological eloquence to wave his fist in front of their faces and shout "Cowardly!" does not appeal to me as a particularly brave act.

Cold-blooded? Why? Because they planned and schemed. Yes. But here are the officers of justice, so-called, with all the power of the State, with all the influence of the press to fan this community into a frenzy of hate, who for months have been planning, scheming, contriving, working to take these two boys' lives. You may stand them up on the trapdoor of the scaffold, and choke them to death, but that act will be infinitely more cold-blooded, whether justified or not, than any act that these boys have committed or can commit

I have heard this crime described, this most distressing and unfortunate homicide, as I would call it, this cold-blooded murder, as the State would call it. I call it a homicide particularly distressing because I am defending. They call it a cold-blooded murder because they want to take human lives. Call it what you will.

Now, your Honor, I have been practicing law a good deal longer than I should have anyhow, for forty-five or forty-six years, and during a part of that time I have tried a good many criminal cases, always defending. It does not mean that I am better. It probably means that I am more squeamish than the other fellows. It means neither that I am better nor worse. It means the way I am made. I can not help it. And I have never yet tried a case where the State's Attorney did not say that it was the most cold-blooded, inexcusable, premeditated case that ever occurred. If it was murder, there never was such a murder. If it was robbery, there never was such a robbery. If it was a conspiracy, it was the most terrible conspiracy that had happened since the Star Chamber passed into oblivion. I am speaking moderately. All of them are the worst. Why? Well, it adds to the credit of the State's Attorneys to be connected with a big case. That is one thing. They can say, "Well, I tried

The Loeb-Leopold Case

the most cold-blooded murder case that ever was tried, and I convicted them, and they are dead." "I tried the worst forgery case that ever was tried, and I won that. I never did anything that was not big." Lawyers are apt to say that.

And then there is another thing, your Honor: these adjectives always go well with juries — *bloody, cold-blooded, despicable, cowardly, dastardly, cruel, heartless.* The twelve jurors, being good themselves, think it is a tribute to their virtue if they follow the litany of the State's Attorney.

I suppose it may have some effect with the court, I do not know. Anyway, those are the chances we take when we do our best to save life and reputation. "How does a judge dare to refuse to hang by the neck until dead two cowardly ruffians who committed the coldest-blooded murder in the history of the world?" That is a good talking point.

They say that this was a cruel murder, the worst that ever happened. I say that very few murders ever occurred that were as free from cruelty as this under all fair rules of measurement.

Of course your Honor, I admit that I hate killing, and I hate it no matter how it is done, whether you shoot a man through the heart, or cut his head off with an axe, or kill him with a chisel, or tie a rope around his neck. I hate it. I always did. I always shall.

But there are degrees, and if I might be permitted to make my own rules I would say that if I were estimating what was the most cruel murder, I might first consider the sufferings of the victim. Now, probably the State would not take that rule. They would say the one that had the most attention in the newspapers. In that way they have got me beaten at the start.

Bobby Franks suffered very little. There is no excuse for his killing. If to hang these two boys would bring him back to life, I would say let them go, and I believe their parents would say so, too. But

> The moving finger writes, and having writ,
> Moves on, nor all your piety nor wit
>   Shall lure it back to cancel half a line,
> Nor all your tears wash out a word of it

Robert Franks is dead, and we cannot call him back to life. It was all over in fifteen minutes after he got into the car, and he probably never knew it or thought of it. That does not justify it. It is the last thing I would do. I am sorry for the poor boy. I am sorry for his parents. But, it is done.

First, I put the victim, who ought not to suffer; next, I would put the attitude of those who kill. What was the attitude of these two boys? It may be that the State's Attorney would think that it was particularly cruel to the victim because he was a boy. Well, my clients are boys, too, and if it would make more serious the offense to kill a boy, it should make less serious the offense of the boys who did the killing.

The Loeb-Leopold Case

This is a senseless, useless, purposeless act of two boys. Now, let me see if I can prove it. There was not a particle of hate, not a grain of malice, there was no opportunity to be cruel except as death is cruel — and death is cruel. There was absolutely no reason in it all, and no motive for it all.

In order to make this the most cruel thing that ever happened of course they must have a motive. And what do they say was the motive? "The motive was to get ten thousand dollars" they say. And they would have you believe they did it to get the money because they were gamblers and needed it to pay gambling debts.

What did Judge Crowe prove? He put on one witness, and one only, who had played bridge with both of them in college, and he said they played for five cents a point. Now, I trust your Honor knows better than I do how much of a game that would be. At poker I might guess, but I know little about bridge.

But what else? He said that in a game one of them lost ninety dollars to the other. They were playing against each other, and one of them lost ninety dollars. Ninety dollars!

It would be trifling excepting, your Honor, that we are dealing in human life. And we are dealing in more than that, we are dealing in the future fate of two families. We are talking of placing a blot upon the escutcheon of two houses that do not deserve it for nothing.

Did they need the money? At that time Richard Loeb had a three thousand dollar checking account in the bank. He had three Liberty Bonds, one of which was past due, and the interest on none had been collected for three years.

In addition to that we brought his father's private secretary here, who swears that whenever he asked for it he got a check, without ever consulting the father. She had an open order to give him a check whenever he wanted it, and she had sent him a check in February, and he had lost it. So he got another in March.

How about Leopold? Leopold was in regular receipt of one hundred and twenty-five dollars a month, he had an automobile, paid nothing for board and clothes, and expenses, he got money whenever he wanted it, and he had arranged to go to Europe and had bought his ticket and was going to leave about the time he was arrested in this case. He passed his examination for the Harvard Law School, and was going to take a short trip to Europe before it was time for him to attend the fall term. His ticket had been bought, and his father was to give him three thousand dollars to make the trip.

In addition to that, these boys' families were extremely wealthy. The boys had been reared in luxury, they had never been denied anything, no want or desire left unsatisfied, no debts, no need of money. And yet they murdered a little boy, against whom they had nothing in the world, without malice, without reason, to get five thousand dollars each

That is what this case rests on. It could not stand up a minute without motive. Without it, it was the senseless act of immature and diseased children as it was, a senseless act of children, wandering around in the dark and moved by some emotion that we still perhaps have not the knowledge or the insight into life to thoroughly understand

Mr Marshall argues to this court that you can do no such thing as to grant us the almost divine favor of saving the lives of two boys, that it is against the law, that the penalty for murder is death, and this court, who in the fiction of the lawyers and the judges, forgets that he is a human being and becomes a court, pulseless, emotionless, devoid of those common feelings which alone make men, that this court as a human machine must hang them because they killed

Now, let us see I do not need to ask mercy from this court for these clients, nor for anybody else, nor for myself, though I have never yet found a person who did not need it But I do not ask mercy for these boys Your Honor may be as strict in the enforcement of the law as you please and you cannot hang these boys You can only hang them because back of the law and back of justice and back of the common instincts of man, and back of the human feeling for the young, is the hoarse

The Loeb-Leopold Case

voice of the mob which says, "Kill." I need ask nothing. What is the law of Illinois?

If one is found guilty of murder in the first degree by a jury, or if he pleads guilty before a court, the court or jury may do one of three things: hang, imprison for life, imprison for a term of not less than fourteen years. Why was this law passed? Undoubtedly in recognition of the growing feeling in all the forward-thinking people of the United States against capital punishment. Undoubtedly through the deep reluctance of courts and juries to take human life.

Your Honor must make the choice, and you have the same right to make one choice as another, no matter what Mr. Justice Blackstone says. It is your Honor's province, you may do it, and I need ask nothing in order to have you do it. There is the statute. But there is more than that in this case.

There was neither cruelty to the deceased, beyond taking his life — which is much — nor was there any depth of guilt and depravity on the part of the defendants, for it was a truly motiveless act, without the slightest feeling of hatred or revenge, done by a couple of children for no sane reason.

But, your Honor, we have gone further than that, and we have sought to show you, as I think we have, the condition of these boys' minds. Of course it is not an easy task to find out the condition of another person's mind. These experts in the main have told

The Loeb-Leopold Case

you that it is impossible to ascertain what the mind is, to start with, or to tell how it acts

There is some evidence somewhere in this record that on their way home from Ann Arbor they began to discuss this question of committing a perfect crime, which had been their phantasy for months The typewriter had nothing whatever to do with it, but to make it seem that they were schemers and planners, that they knew how to think and how to act, it is argued that they went all the way to Ann Arbor in the nighttime to steal a typewriter, instead of buying one here, or stealing one here, or getting one here, or using their own, or advertising for one, or securing one in any of a hundred ways

Of course it is impossible on the face of it, but let us see what the evidence is. They did bring a typewriter from Ann Arbor and on that typewriter they wrote these letters, and after the boy had been killed they threw the typewriter into the lagoon, after twisting off the letters Why did they twist off the letters? Well, I suppose anybody knows why. Because one who is fairly familiar with a typewriter knows that you can always detect the writing on almost every typewriter There will be imperfect letters, imperfect tracking and imperfect this, that and the other, by which detection is accomplished, and probably they knew it

But mark this Leopold kept this typewriter in his house for six months According to the testimony of the maid, he had written many letters on it

The Loeb-Leopold Case

According to the testimony of his tutors he had written the dope sheets for his law examination on it, numbers of them. These were still in existence. The State's Attorney got them, the typewriter could be identified without the machine at all. It was identified without the machine, all that was needed was to show that the same machine that wrote the ransom letter wrote the dope sheets and wrote the other letters.

No effort was made to conceal it through all these months. All the boys' friends knew it, the maid knew it, everybody in the house knew it. Were they trying to conceal it? Did they take a drive in the nighttime to Ann Arbor to get it, together with other stuff so that they might be tracked, or did they just get it with other stuff without any thought of this homicide that happened six months later?

The State says, in order to make out the wonderful mental processes of these two boys that they fixed up a plan to go to Ann Arbor to get this machine. And yet, when they got ready to do this act, they went down the street a few doors from their house and bought a rope, they went around the corner and bought acid, then went somewhere else and bought tape, they went down to the hotel and rented a room, and then gave it up, and went to another hotel and rented one there. And then Dick Loeb went to the hotel room, took a valise containing his library card and some books from the library, left it two days in the room, until the hotel took the valise and took the books Then he went to another hotel and rented another room He might just as well have sent his card with the ransom letter

Were these boys normal? Here were two boys with good intellect, one eighteen and one nineteen They had all the prospects that life could hold out for any of the young, one a graduate of Chicago and another of Ann Arbor, one who had passed his examination for the Harvard Law School and was about to take a trip in Europe, another who had passed at Ann Arbor, the youngest in his class, with three thousand dollars in the bank boys who could reach any position that was given to boys of that kind to reach, boys of distinguished and honorable families, families of wealth and position, with all the world before them And they gave it all up for nothing For nothing!

How insane they are I care not, whether medically or legally They did not reason, they could not reason, they committed the most foolish, most unprovoked, most causeless act that any two boys ever committed, and they put themselves where the rope is dangling above their heads Why did they kill little Bobby Franks? Not for money, not for spite, not for hate. They killed him as they might kill a spider or a fly, for the experience They killed him because they were made that way Because somewhere in the infinite processes that go to the making up of the boy or the man something slipped, and those unfortunate lads sit here hated, despised, outcasts, with the community shouting for their blood

I heard the State's Attorney talk of mothers. Mr. Savage is talking for the mothers, and Mr. Crowe is thinking of the mothers, and I am thinking of the mothers. Mr. Savage, with the immaturity of youth and inexperience, says that if we hang them there will be no more killing. This world has been one long slaughterhouse from the beginning until today, and killing goes on and on and on, and will forever.

Kill them. Will that prevent other senseless boys or other vicious men or vicious women from killing? No! It will simply call upon every weak-minded person to do as they have done. I know how easy it is to talk about mothers when you want to do something cruel. But I am thinking of the mothers, too. I know that any mother might be the mother of a little Bobby Franks, who left his home and went to his school, and who never came back. I know that any mother might be the mother of a Richard Loeb and a Nathan Leopold, just the same. The trouble is this, that if she is the mother of a Nathan Leopold or of a Richard Loeb, she has to ask herself the question " How came my children to be what they are? From what ancestry did they get this strain? How far removed was the poison that destroyed their lives? Was I the bearer of the seed that brings them to death?"

Any mother might be the mother of any of them. But these two are the victims. I remember a little poem that gives the soliloquy of a boy about to be hanged, a soliloquy such as these boys might make

> The night my father got me
>   His mind was not on me,
> He did not plague his fancy
>   To muse if I should be
>   The son you see
>
> The day my mother bore me
>   She was a fool and glad,
> For all the pain I cost her,
>   That she had borne the lad
>   That borne she had
>
> My father and my mother
>   Out of the light they lie,
> The warrant would not find them,
>   And here, 'tis only I
>   Shall hang so high
>
> O let not man remember
>   The soul that God forgot,
> But fetch the county sheriff
>   And noose me in a knot,
>   And I will rot
>
> And so the game is ended,
>   That should not have begun
> My father and my mother
>   They had a likely son,
>   And I have none

No one knows what will be the fate of the child he gets or the child she bears, the fate of the child

The Loeb-Leopold Case

is the last thing considered. This weary old world goes on, begetting, with birth and with living and with death, and all of it is blind from the beginning to the end. I do not know what it was that made these boys do this mad act, but I do know there is a reason for it. I know they did not beget themselves. I know that any one of an infinite number of causes reaching back to the beginning might be working out in these boys' minds, whom you are asked to hang because some one in the past has sinned against them.

I am sorry for the fathers as well as the mothers, for the fathers who give their strength and their lives for educating and protecting and creating a fortune for the boys that they love, for the mothers who go down into the shadow of death for their children, who nourish them and care for them, and risk their lives, that they may live, who watch them with tenderness and fondness and longing, and who go down into dishonor and disgrace for the children that they love.

All of these are helpless. We are all helpless. But when you are pitying the father and the mother of poor Bobby Franks, what about the fathers and mothers of these two unfortunate boys, and what about the unfortunate boys themselves, and what about all the fathers and all the mothers and all the boys and all the girls who tread a dangerous maze in darkness from birth to death?

The Loeb-Leopold Case

What is my friend's idea of justice? He says to this court, whom he says he respects — and I believe he does — your Honor, who sits here patiently, holding the lives of these two boys in your hands "Give them the same mercy that they gave to Bobby Franks"

Is that the law? Is that justice? Is this what a court should do? Is this what a State's Attorney should do? If the State in which I live is not kinder, more humane, more considerate, more intelligent than the mad act of these two boys, I am sorry that I have lived so long.

I am sorry for all fathers and all mothers. The mother who looks into the blue eyes of her little babe cannot help musing over the end of the child, whether it will be crowned with the greatest promises which her mind can image or possibly meet death upon the scaffold All she can do is to rear him with love and care, to watch over him tenderly, to meet life with hope and trust and confidence, and to leave the rest with fate

Without any excuse, without the slightest motive, not moved by money, not moved by passion, by nothing except the vague wanderings of children, these boys rented a machine, and about four o'clock in the afternoon started to find somebody to kill They went over to the Harvard School Dick's little brother was there, on the playground Dick went there himself in open daylight, known by all of them, he had been a pupil there himself, the school was near his home, and he looked over the little boys

Your Honor has been in these courts for a long time, you have listened to murder cases before Has any such case ever appeared here or in any of the books? Has it ever come to the human experience of any judge, or any lawyer? Never once!

They first picked out a little boy named Levinson, and Dick trailed him around Now, of course, that is a hard story It is a story that shocks one A boy bent on killing, not knowing where he would go or whom he would get, but seeking some victim Here is a little boy, but the circumstances are not opportune, and so he fails to get him

Dick abandons that lead, Dick and Nathan are in the car, and they see Bobby Franks on the street, and they call to him to get into the car It is about five o'clock in the afternoon, in the long summer days, on a thickly settled street, built up with homes, the houses of their friends and their companions, automobiles appearing and disappearing, and they take him in the car

If there had been a question of revenge, yes, if there had been a question of hate, where no one cares for his own fate, intent only on accomplishing his end, yes But without any motive or any reason they picked up this little boy right in sight of their own homes, and surrounded by their neighbors They drive a little way, on a populous street, where

The Loeb-Leopold Case

everybody could see, where eyes might be at every window as they pass by. They hit him over the head with a chisel and kill him.

They pull the dead boy into the back seat, and wrap him in a blanket, and this funeral car starts on its route. If ever any death car went over the same route or the same kind of a route, driven by sane people, I have never heard of it, and I fancy no one else has ever heard of it. This car is driven for twenty miles. First down through thickly populated streets, where everyone knew the boys and their families, and had known them for years, till they come to the Midway Boulevard.

The slightest accident, the slightest misfortune, a bit of curiosity, an arrest for speeding, anything would bring destruction. They go down the Midway, through the park, meeting hundreds of machines, in sight of thousands of eyes, with the dead boy. They go down a thickly populated street through South Chicago, and then for three miles take the longest street to go through this city, built solid with business buildings, filled with automobiles backed upon the street, with street cars on the track, with thousands of peering eyes, Leopold driving and Loeb on the back seat, with the corpse of little Bobby Franks, the blood streaming from him, wetting everything in the car.

Nothing I know of can compare with it except the mad acts of the fool in *King Lear*.

And yet they tell me that this is sanity, they tell

me that the brains of these boys are not diseased. You need no experts, you need no X-rays, you need no study of the endocrines. They get through South Chicago, and they take the regular automobile road down toward Hammond. There is the same situation, hundreds of machines, any accident might encompass their ruin. They stop at the forks of the road, and leave little Bobby Franks, soaked with blood, in the machine, and get their dinner, and eat it without an emotion or a qualm.

But we are told that they planned. Well, a maniac plans, an idiot plans, an animal plans, any brain that functions may plan, but their plans were the diseased plans of the diseased mind.

And still, your Honor, on account of its weirdness and its strangeness, and its advertising, we are forced to fight. For what? Forced to plead to this court that two boys, one eighteen and the other nineteen, may be permitted to live in silence and solitude and disgrace and spend all their days in the penitentiary.

I can not understand it, your Honor. It would be past belief, excepting that to the four corners of the earth the news of this weird act has been carried, and the intellect has been stifled, and men have been controlled by passions which should have died centuries ago.

My friend Savage pictured to you the putting of this dead boy in this culvert. Well, no one can minutely describe any killing and not make it shocking. It is shocking because we love life and because we instinctively draw back from death It is shocking wherever it is and however it is, and perhaps all death is almost equally shocking

But here is the picture of a dead boy, past pain, when no harm can come to him, put in a culvert, after taking off his clothes so that the evidence would be destroyed, and that is pictured to this court as a reason for hanging Well, your Honor, that does not appeal to me as strongly as the hitting over the head of little Robert Franks with a chisel. The boy was dead

Your Honor, I can think of another scene I can think, and only *think*, your Honor, of taking two boys, one eighteen and the other nineteen, irresponsible, weak, diseased, penning them in a cell checking off the days and the hours and the minutes, until they will be taken out and hanged Wouldn't it be a glorious day for Chicago? Wouldn't it be a glorious triumph for the State's Attorney? Wouldn't it be a glorious illustration of Christianity and kindness and charity? I can picture them, wakened in the gray light of morning, furnished a *suit of clothes by the State, led to the scaffold, their feet tied, black caps drawn over their heads, stood on a trapdoor, the hangman pressing a spring, so that it gives way under them, I can see them fall through space — and — stopped by the rope around their necks.

This would surely expiate placing Bobby Franks in the culvert after he was dead This would doubtless bring immense satisfaction to some people. It would bring a greater satisfaction because it would be done in the name of justice. I am always suspicious of "righteous indignation." Nothing is more cruel than "righteous indignation." To hear young men talk glibly of justice!

If there were such a thing as justice it could only be administered by those who knew the inmost thoughts of the man to whom they were meting it out. Aye, who knew the father and mother and the grandparents and the infinite number of people back of him, who knew the origin of every cell that went into the body, who could understand the structure, and how it acted, who could tell how the emotions that sway the human being affected that particular frail piece of clay. It means more than that. It means that you must appraise every influence that moves them, the civilization where they live, and all society which enters into the making of the child or the man! If your Honor can do it — if you can do it you are wise, and with wisdom goes mercy.

No one with wisdom and with understanding, no one who is honest with himself and with his own life, whoever he may be, no one who has seen himself the prey and the sport and the plaything of the infinite forces that move man, no one who has tried and who has failed — and we have all tried and we have all failed — no one can tell what justice is for some one else or for himself — and the more he tries and the more responsibility he takes the more he clings to mercy as being the one thing which he is sure should control his judgment of men

For life! Where is the human heart that would not be satisfied with that? Where is the one who understands his own life and who has a particle of feeling that could ask for more? Any cry for more roots back to the hyena, it roots back to the hissing serpent it roots back to the beast and the jungle It is not a part of that feeling of mercy and pity and understanding of each other which we believe has been slowly raising man from his low estate It is not a part of the finer instincts which are slow to develop, of the wider knowledge which is slow to come, and slow to move us when it comes It is not a part of all that makes the best there is in man It is not a part of all that promises any hope for the future and any justice for the present And must I ask that these boys get mercy by spending the rest of their lives in prison, year following year, month following month and day following day, with nothing to look forward to but hostile guards and stone walls? It ought not to be hard to get that much mercy in any court in the year 1924

These boys left this body down in the culvert and they came back

They got their dinners They parked the bloody automobile in front of Leopold's house They cleaned it to some extent that night and left it standing in the street in front of their home

"Oriented," of course "Oriented" They left

it there for the night, so that anybody might see and might know They took it into the garage the next day and washed it, and then poor little Dickie Loeb — I shouldn't call him Dickie, and I shouldn't call him poor, because that might be playing for sympathy, and you have no right to ask for sympathy in this world You should ask for justice, whatever that may be, and only State's Attorneys know

And then in a day or so we find Dick Loeb with his pockets stuffed with newspapers telling of the Franks tragedy We find him consulting with his friends in the club, with the newspaper reporters, and my experience is that the last person that a conscious criminal associates with is a reporter He even shuns them more than he does a detective, because they are smarter and less merciful But he picks up a reporter, and he tells him he has read a great many detective stories, and he knows just how this would happen and that the fellow who telephoned must have been down on 63rd Street, and the way to find him is to go down on 63rd Street and visit the drug stores, and he would go with him

And Dick Loeb pilots reporters around the drug stores where the telephoning was done, and he talks about it, and he takes the newspapers with him, and he is having a glorious time

Talk about scheming Yes, it is the scheme of disease, it is the scheme of infancy, it is the scheme of fools, it is the scheme of irresponsibility from the time it was conceived until the last act in the tragedy.

Many a time has mercy come even from the State's Attorney's office. And yet, forsooth, for some reason, here is a case of two immature boys of diseased mind, as plain as the light of day, and they say you can get justice only by shedding their last drop of blood!

Why? Why? It is unheard of, unprecedented in this court, unknown among civilized men. And yet this court is to make an example or civilization will fail. I suppose civilization will survive if your Honor hangs them. But your Honor will be turning back over the long, long road we have traveled. Your Honor would be turning back to the days which Brother Marshall seems to love, when they burned people thirteen years of age. You would be dealing a staggering blow to all that has been done in the city of Chicago in the last twenty years for the protection of infancy and childhood and youth.

And for what? Because the people are talking about it. It would not mean, your Honor, that your reason was convinced. It would mean in this land of ours, where talk is cheap, where newspapers are plentiful, where the most immature expresses his opinion, and the more immature the stronger, that a court couldn't help feeling the great pressure of the public opinion which they say exists in this case.

Coming alone in this court room with obscure defendants, doing what has been done in this case, coming with the outside world shut off, as in most cases, and saying to this court and counsel, " I believe that these boys ought not to be at large, I believe they are immature and irresponsible, and I am willing to enter a plea of guilty and let you sentence them to life imprisonment," how long do you suppose your Honor would hesitate? Do you suppose the State's Attorneys would raise their voices in protest?

If a man could judge a fellow in coldness without taking account of his own life, without taking account of what he knows of human life, without some understanding, how long would we be a race of real human beings? It has taken the world a long time for man to get even where he is today If the law was administered without any feeling of sympathy or humanity or kindliness, we would begin our long, slow journey back to the jungle that was formerly our home

Three hundred and forty murder cases in ten years with pleas of guilty in this county One hanging on a plea of guilty, and that a man forty years of age And yet they say we come here with a preposterous plea for mercy When did any plea for mercy become preposterous in any tribunal in all the universe?

This tragedy has not claimed all the attention it has had, your Honor, on account of its atrocity What is it? There are two reasons, and only two that I can see. First is the reputed extreme wealth

The Loeb-Leopold Case

of these families, not only the Loeb and Leopold families, but the Franks family, and of course it is unusual. And next is the fact it is weird and uncanny and motiveless. That is what attracted the attention of the world. Many may say now that they want to hang these boys, but I know that giving the people blood is something like giving them their dinner. When they get it they go to sleep. They may for the time being have an emotion, but they will bitterly regret it. And I undertake to say that if these two boys are sentenced to death, and are hanged, on that day there will be a pall over the people of this land that will be dark and deep, and at least cover every humane and intelligent person with its gloom. I wonder if it will do good. I wonder if it will help the children — and there are many like these.

What about this matter of crime and punishment, anyhow? I may know less than the rest, but I have at least tried to find out, and I am fairly familiar with the best literature that has been written on that subject in the last hundred years. The more men study, the more they doubt the effect of severe punishment on crime. And yet Mr. Savage tells this court that if these boys are hanged, there will be no more murder. Mr. Savage is an optimist. He says that if the defendants are hanged there will be no more boys like these.

I could give him a sketch of punishment, punishment beginning with the brute which killed some-

The Loeb-Leopold Case

thing because something hurt it, the punishment of the savage, if a person is injured in the tribe, they must injure somebody in the other tribe; if one is killed his friends or family must kill in return

You can trace it all down through the history of man. You can trace the burnings, the boilings, the drawings and quarterings, the hanging of people in England at the crossroads, carving them up and hanging them as examples for all to see

We can come down to the last century when nearly two hundred crimes were punishable by death and by death in every form, not only hanging — that was too humane — but burning, boiling, cutting into pieces, torturing in all conceivable forms

You can read the stories of the hangings on a high hill, and the populace for miles around coming out to the scene, that everybody might be awed into goodness. Hanging for picking pockets — and more pockets were picked in the crowd that went to the hanging than had been known before. Hangings for murder — and men were murdered on the way there and on the way home. Hangings for poaching, hangings for everything, and hangings in public, not shut up cruelly and brutally in a jail, out of the light of day, wakened in the nighttime and led forth and killed, but taken to the shire town on a high hill, in the presence of a multitude, so that all might see that the wages of sin were death

What happened? I have read the life of Lord Shaftesbury, a great nobleman of England, who gave his life and his labors toward modifying the penal code. I have read of the slow, painful efforts through all the ages for more humanity of man to his fellow man. I know what history says, I know what it means, and I know what flows from it, so far as we can tell, which is not with certainty.

I know that every step in the progress of humanity has been met and opposed by prosecutors, and many times by courts. I know that when petty larceny was punishable by death in England juries refused to convict. They were too humane to obey the law, and judges refused to sentence. I know that when the delusion of witchcraft was spreading over Europe many a judge so shaped his cases that no crime of witchcraft could be punished in his court. I know that these trials were stopped in America because juries would no longer convict. I know that every step in the progress of the world in reference to crime has come from that deep well of sympathy, that in spite of all our training and all our conventions and all our teaching, still lives in the human breast.

Gradually the laws have been changed and modified, and men look back with horror at the hangings and the killings of the past. What did they find in England? That as they got rid of these barbarous statutes crimes decreased instead of increased, as the criminal law was modified and humanized, there was less crime instead of more. I will undertake to say, your Honor, that you can scarcely find a single book written by a student — and I will include all the works on criminology of the past — that has not made the statement over and over again that as the penal code was made less terrible, crimes grew less frequent

If these two boys die on the scaffold, which I can never bring myself to imagine, if they do die on the scaffold, the details of this will be spread over the world. Every newspaper in the United States will carry a full account. Every newspaper of Chicago will be filled with the gruesome details. It will enter every home and every family.

Will it make men better or make men worse? How many will be colder and crueler for it? How many will enjoy the details? And you cannot enjoy human suffering without being affected for the worse.

What influence will it have upon the millions of men who will read it? What influence will it have upon the millions of women who will read it, more sensitive, more impressionable, more imaginative than men? What influence will it have upon the infinite number of children who will devour its details as Dickie Loeb has enjoyed reading detective stories? What influence, let me ask you, will it have for the unborn babes still sleeping in their mother's womb? And what influence will it have on the psychology of the fathers and mothers yet to come? Do I need to argue to your Honor that cruelty only breeds cruelty, that hatred only causes hatred, that if there is any way to soften this human heart, which is hard enough at its best, if there is any way to kill evil and hatred and all that goes with it, it is not through evil and hatred and cruelty? It is through charity and love and understanding

How often do people need to be told this? Look back at the world There is not a philosopher, not a religious leader, not a creed that has not taught it. This is a Christian community, at least it boasts of it. Let me ask this court, is there any doubt about whether these boys would be safe in the hands of the founder of the Christian religion? It would be blasphemy to say they would not Nobody could imagine, nobody could even think of it.

Your Honor, I feel like apologizing for urging it so long It is not because I doubt this court It is not because I do not know something of the human emotions and the human heart. It is not that I do not know that every result of logic, every page of history, every line of philosophy and religion, and every precedent in this court, urge this court to save life It is not that I have become obsessed with this deep feeling of hate and anger that has swept across this city and this land. I have been fighting it, battling with it, until it has fairly driven me mad, until I sometimes wonder whether every righteous human emotion has not gone down in the raging storm

I am not pleading so much for these boys as I am for the infinite number of others to follow, those who perhaps cannot be as well defended as these have been, those who may go down in the tempest, without aid. It is of them I am thinking, and for them I am begging of this court not to turn backward toward the barbarous and cruel past.

Now, your Honor, who are these two boys? Leopold, with a wonderfully brilliant mind, Loeb, with an unusual intelligence, both from their very youth crowded like hothouse plants, to learn more and more and more. Dr. Krohn says that they are intelligent. In spite of that, it is true they are unusually intelligent. But it takes something besides brains to make a human being who can adjust himself to life.

In fact, as Dr. Church and Dr. Singer regretfully admitted, brains are not the chief essential in human conduct. There is no question about it. The emotions are the urge that makes us live, the urge that makes us work or play, or move along the pathways of life. They are the instinctive things. In fact, intellect is a late development of life. Long before it was evolved, the emotional life kept the organism in existence until death. Whatever our action is, it comes from the emotions, and nobody is balanced without them.

Four or five years ago the world was startled by a story about a boy of eleven, the youngest boy ever turned out at Harvard, who had studied everything on earth and understood it. All questions of science and philosophy he could discuss with the most learned How he got it nobody knows It was prophesied that he would have a brilliant future In a short time the fire had burned out He was a prodigy, with nothing but this marvelous brain power, which nobody understood or could understand He was an intellectual freak He never was a boy, he never will be a normal man

We have all read of Blind Tom, who was an idiot, and yet a marvelous musician He never could understand music, and he never did understand it, he never knew anything about it, and yet he could go to the piano and play so well that people marveled and wondered How it comes nobody can explain

The question of intellect means the smallest part of life Back of this are man's nerves, muscles, heart, blood, lungs — in fact, the whole organism, the brain is the least part in human development. Without the emotion-life man is nothing All teaching and all training appeal, not only to the intellectual, but to emotional life

A child is born with plastic brain, ready for such impressions as come to it Gradually his parents and his teachers tell him things, teach him habits, show him that he may do this and he may not do that, teach him the difference between his and mine No child knows this when he is born He knows nothing about property or property rights They are given to him as he goes along He is like the animal that wants something and goes out and gets it, kills it, operating purely from instinct, without training. The child is gradually taught, and habits are built up. These habits are supposed to be strong enough so that they will form inhibitions against conduct when the emotions come in conflict with the duties of life.

Dr. Singer and Dr. Church admitted exactly what I am saying now. The child of himself knows nothing about right and wrong, and the teachings built up give him habits, so he will be able to control certain instincts that surge upon him, and which surge upon everyone who lives. If the instinct is strong enough and the habit weak enough, the habit goes down before it. His conduct depends upon the relative strength of the instinct and the habit that has been built up.

Education means fixing these habits so deeply in the life of man that they stand him in stead when he needs them to keep him in the path — and that is all it does mean. Suppose one sees a thousand-dollar bill and nobody present. He may have the impulse to take it. If he does not take it, it will be because his emotional nature revolts at it, through habit and through training. If the emotional nature does not revolt at it he will do it. That is why people do not commit what we call crime, that, and caution. All education means is the building of habits so that certain conduct revolts you and stops you, saves you, but without an emotional nature you cannot do that. Some are born practically without it.

On Sunday, June 1st, before any of the friends

of these boys or their counsel could see them, while they were in the care of the State's Attorney's office, they brought them in to be examined by their alienists Dr Patrick said that they had no emotional reactions Dr Church said the same These are their alienists, not ours These boys could tell this gruesome story without a change of countenance, without the slightest feelings. What was the reason? I do not know I know what causes the emotional life I know it comes from the nerves, the muscles, the endocrine glands, the vegetative system I know it is the most important part of life

Is Dickie Loeb to blame because out of the infinite forces that conspired to form him, the forces that were at work producing him ages before he was born, because out of these infinite combinations he was born without it? If he is, then there should be a new definition for justice Is he to blame for what he did not have and never had? Is he to blame that his machine is imperfect? Who is to blame? I do not know I have never in my life been interested so much in fixing blame as I have in relieving people from blame. I am not wise enough to fix it I know that somewhere in the past that entered into him something missed It may be defective nerves. It may be a defective heart or liver It may be defective endocrine glands I know it is something I know that nothing happens in this world without a cause I know, your Honor, that if you, sitting here in this court, and in this case, had infinite knowledge you could lay your fingers on it, and I know you would not visit it on Dickie Loeb. I asked Dr. Church and I asked Dr. Singer whether, if they were wise enough to know they could not find the cause, and both of them said yes.

There are at least two theories of man's responsibility. There may be more. There is the old theory that if a man does something it is because he willfully, purposely, maliciously and with a malignant heart sees fit to do it. And that goes back to the possession of man by devils. The old indictments used to read that a man being possessed of a devil did so and so. But why was he possessed with the devil? Did he invite him in? Could he help it? Very few half-civilized people believe that doctrine any more. Science has been at work, humanity has been at work, scholarship has been at work, and intelligent people now know that every human being is the product of the endless heredity back of him and the infinite environment around him. He is made as he is and he is the sport of all that goes before him and is applied to him, and under the same stress and storm you would act one way, I another, and poor Dickie Loeb another.

Take a normal boy your Honor. Do you suppose he could have taken a boy into an automobile without any reason and hit him over the head and killed him? I might just as well ask you whether you thought the sun could shine at midnight in this latitude. It is not a part of normality. Something was wrong I am asking your Honor not to visit the grave and dire and terrible misfortunes of Dickie Loeb and Nathan Leopold upon these two boys. I do not know where to place it. I know it is somewhere in the infinite economy of nature, and if I were wise enough I could find it. I know it is there, and to say that because they are as they are you should hang them, is brutality and cruelty, and savors of the fang and claw.

Every one of the alienists on both sides has told this court, what no doubt this court already knew, that the emotions furnish the urge and the drive to life. A man can get along without his intellect, and most people do, but he cannot get along without his emotions. He eats and he drinks, he works and plays and sleeps, in obedience to his emotional system. The intellectual part of man acts only as a judge over his emotions, and then he generally gets it wrong, and has to rely on his instincts to save him.

These boys — I do not care what their mentality — that simply makes it worse — are emotionally defective. Every single alienist who has testified in this case has said so. The only person who did not was Dr Krohn. While I am on that subject, lest I forget the eminent doctor, I want to refer to one or two things. In the first place, all these alienists that the State called came into the State's Attorney's office and heard these boys tell their story of this crime, and that is all they heard.

The Loeb-Leopold Case

Now, your Honor is familiar with Chicago the same as I am, and I am willing to admit right here and now that the two ablest alienists in Chicago are Dr Church and Dr Patrick. There may be abler ones, but we lawyers do not know them

And I will go further if my friend Crowe had not got to them first, I would have tried to get them We could not get them, and Mr Crowe was very wise, and he deserves a great deal of credit for the industry, the research and the thoroughness that he and his staff have used in detecting this terrible crime He worked with intelligence and rapidity If here and there he trampled on the edges of the Constitution I am not going to talk about it here If he did it, he is not the first one in that office and probably will not be the last who will do it, so let that go A great many people in this world believe the end justifies the means I don't know but that I do myself And that is the reason I never want to take the side of the prosecution, because I might harm an individual I am sure the State will live anyhow.

On that Sunday afternoon, before we had a chance, he got in two alienists, Church and Patrick, and also called Dr. Krohn, and they sat around hearing these boys tell their stories, and that is all Your Honor, they were not holding an examination. It has not the slightest earmarks of an examination for sanity It was just an inquest; a little premature, but still an inquest

What is the truth about it? What did Patrick say? He said that it was not a good opportunity for examination. What did Church say? I read from his own book what was necessary for an examination, and he said that it was not a good opportunity for an examination. What did Krohn say? "Fine — a fine opportunity for an examination," the best he had ever heard of, or that ever anybody had, because their souls were stripped naked. Krohn is not an alienist. He is an orator.

Patrick and Church said that the conditions were unfavorable for an examination, that they never would choose it, that their opportunities were poor. And yet Krohn states the contrary — Krohn, who for sixteen years has not been a physician, but has used a license for the sake of haunting these courts, civil and criminal, and going up and down the land peddling perjury.

What else did he say, in which the State's alienists dispute him? Both of them say that these boys showed no adequate emotion. Krohn said they did. One boy fainted. They had been in the hands of the State's Attorney for sixty hours. They had been in the hands of policemen, lawyers, detectives, stenographers, inquisitors and newspaper men for sixty hours, and one of them fainted. Well, the only person who is entirely without emotion is a dead man. You cannot live without breathing and some emotional responses. Krohn says "Why, Loeb had emotion, he was polite, begged our pardon, got up

The Loeb-Leopold Case

from his chair." Even Dr. Krohn knows better than that. I fancy if your Honor goes into an elevator where there is a lady he takes off his hat. Is that out of emotion for the lady or is it habit? You say, "Please," and "Thank you," because of habit. Emotions haven't the slightest thing to do with it.

Krohn told the story of this interview and he told almost twice as much as the other two men who sat there and heard it. And how he told it! When he testified my mind carried me back to the time when I was a "kid," which was some years ago, and we used to eat watermelons. I have seen little boys take a rind of watermelon and cover their whole faces with water, eat it, devour it, and have the time of their lives, up to their ears in watermelon. And when I heard Dr. Krohn testify in this case, to take the blood of these two boys, I could see his mouth water with the joy it gave him, and he showed all the delight and pleasure of myself and my young companions when we ate watermelon.

I can imagine a psychiatrist, a real one who knows the mechanism of man, who knows life and its machinery, who knows the misfortunes of youth, who knows the stress and the strain of adolescence which comes to every boy and overpowers so many, who knows the weird fantastic world that hedges around the life of a child — I can imagine a psychiatrist who might honestly think that under the crude definitions of the law the defendants are sane and know the difference between right and wrong

The Loeb-Leopold Case

But if he were a real physician, whose mission is the highest that man can follow, to save life and minister to human suffering — to save life regardless of what the life is — to prevent suffering regardless of whose suffering it is — and no mission could be higher than that — and if he were called on for an opinion that might send his fellow man to doom, I can imagine him doing it reluctantly, carefully, modestly, timorously, fearfully, and being careful that he did not turn one hair to the right or left more than he should, and giving the advantage in favor of life and humanity and mercy, but I can never imagine a real physician who cared for life or who thought of anything excepting cash, gloating over his testimony, as Dr Krohn did in this case

The mind, your Honor, is an illusive thing Whether it exists or not no one can tell It cannot be found as you find the brain Its relation to the brain and the nervous system is uncertain It simply means the activity of the body, which is co-ordinated with the brain But when we do find from human conduct that we believe there is a diseased mind we naturally speculate on how it came about And we wish to find always, if possible, the reason why it is so We may find it; we may not find it, because the unknown is infinitely wider and larger than the known, both as to the human mind and as to almost everything else in the universe

I have tried to study the lives of these two most unfortunate boys Three months ago, if their

The Loeb-Leopold Case

friends and the friends of the family had been asked to pick out the most promising lads of their acquaintance they probably would have picked these two boys. With every opportunity, with plenty of wealth, they would have said that those two would succeed. In a day, by an act of madness, all this is destroyed, until the best they can hope for now is a life of silence and pain, continuing to the end of their years. How did it happen?

Let us take Dickie Loeb first. I do not claim to know how it happened, I have sought to find out. I know that something, or some combination of things, is responsible for his mad act. I know that there are no accidents in nature. I know that effect follows cause.

Can I find what was wrong? I think I can. Here was a boy at a tender age, placed in the hands of a governess, intellectual, vigorous, devoted, with a strong ambition for the welfare of this boy. He was pushed in his studies, as plants are forced in hothouses. He had no pleasures, such as a boy should have, except as they were gained by lying and cheating. Now, I am not criticising the nurse. I suggest that some day your Honor look at her picture. It explains her fully. Forceful, brooking no interference, she loved the boy, and her ambition was that he should reach the highest perfection. No time to pause, no time to stop from one book to another, no time to have those pleasures which a boy ought to have to create a normal life.

And what happened? Your Honor what would happen? Nothing strange or unusual. This nurse was with him all the time, except when he stole out at night, from two to fourteen years of age, and it is instructive to read her letter to show her attitude. It speaks volumes, tells exactly the relation between these two people. He scheming and planning as healthy boys would do, to get out from under her restraint. She putting before him the best books, which children generally do not want, and he, when she was not looking, reading detective stories, which he devoured, story after story, in his young life. Of all of this there can be no question. What is the result? Every story he read was a story of crime. We have a statute in this State, passed only last year, if I recall it, which forbids minors reading stories of crime. The legislature in its wisdom felt that it would produce criminal tendencies in the boys who read them. The legislature of this State has given its opinion, and forbidden boys to read these books. He read them day after day. He never stopped. While he was passing through college at Ann Arbor he was still reading them. When he was a senior he read them, and almost nothing else.

Now, these facts are beyond dispute. He early developed the tendency to mix with crime, to be a detective, as a little boy shadowing people on the street, as a little child going out with his phantasy of being the head of a band of criminals. How did this grow and develop in him? Let us see It seems to me as natural as the day following the night Every detective story is a story of a sleuth getting the best of it, trailing some unfortunate individual through devious ways until his victim is finally landed in jail or stands on the gallows They all show how smart the detective is, and where the criminal himself falls down

This boy early in his life conceived the idea that there could be a crime that nobody could ever detect, that there could be one where the detective did not land his game He had been interested in the story of Charley Ross, who was kidnaped

I might digress here just a moment, because my friend Savage spoke about two crimes that were committed here — kidnaping and murder That is, the court should hang them twice — once for each There are more than two committed here There are more than two crimes committed in almost every capital act

In almost any important crime the State's Attorney can write indictments as long as the paper lasts

He wanted to commit a perfect crime There had been growing in his brain, dwarfed and twisted — as every act in this case shows it to have been dwarfed and twisted — there had been growing this scheme, not due to any wickedness of Dickie Loeb, for he is a child It grew as he grew, it grew from those around him, it grew from the lack of the proper training until it possessed him He believed he could plan the perfect crime He had thought of it and talked of it for years, and then came this sorry act of his, utterly irrational and motiveless, a plan to commit a perfect crime which must contain kidnaping, and there must be ransom, or else it could not be perfect, and they must get the money

The State itself in opening this case said that it was largely for experience and for a thrill, which it was In the end the State switched it on to the foolish reason of getting cash Every fact in this case shows that cash had almost nothing to do with it, except as a factor in the perfect crime

This phantasy grew in the mind of Dickie Loeb almost before he began to read It developed as a child just as kleptomania has developed in many a person and is clearly recognized by the courts He went from one thing to another — in the main insignificant, childish things And, finally, the planning for this crime Murder was the least part of it, to kidnap and get the money, and kill in connection with it, that was the childish scheme growing up in these childish minds And they had it in mind for five or six months — planning what? Planning where every step was foolish and childish, acts that could have been planned in an hour or a day; planning this, and then planning that, changing this and changing that, the weird actions of two mad brains

Counsel have laughed at us for talking about phantasies and hallucinations They have laughed at us in one breath, but admitted it in another Let us look at that for a moment, your Honor Your Honor has been a child I well remember that I have been a child And while youth has its advantages, it has its grievous troubles There is an old prayer, ' Though I grow old in years, let me keep the heart of a child The heart of a child with its abundant life, its disregard for consequences, its living in the moment, and for the moment alone, its lack of responsibility, and its freedom from care

The law knows and has recognized childhood for many and many a long year The brain of the child is the home of dreams, of castles, of visions, of illusions and of delusions In fact, there could be no childhood without delusions, for delusions are always more alluring than facts Delusions, dreams and hallucinations are a part of the warp and woof of childhood You know it and I know it I remember, when I was a child, the men seemed as tall as the trees, the trees as tall as the mountains I can remember very well when, as a little boy, I swam the deepest spot in the river for the first time I swam breathlessly, and landed with as much sense of glory and triumph as Julius Cæsar felt when he led his army across the Rubicon I have been back since, and I can almost step across the same place, but it seemed an ocean then And those men who I thought were so wonderful were dead and left nothing behind I had lived in a dream I had never known the real world which I met, to my discomfort and despair, and that dispelled the illusions of my youth

The whole life of childhood is a dream and an illusion, and whether they take one shape or another shape depends not upon the dreamy boy but on what surrounds him As well might I have dreamed of burglars and wished to be one as to dream of policemen and wished to be one Perhaps I was lucky, too, that I had no money We have grown to think that the misfortune is in not having it The great misfortune in this case is the money That has destroyed these lives That has fostered these illusions That has promoted this mad act And if your Honor shall doom them to die, it will be because they are the sons of the rich

Do you suppose that if they lived up here on the Northwest Side and had no money, with the evidence as clear in this case as it is, any human being would want to hang them? Excessive wealth is a grievous misfortune in every step in life When I read malicious newspapers talking of excessive fees in this case, it makes me ill That there is nothing bigger in life, that it is presumed that no man lives to whom money is not the first concern, that human instincts, sympathy and kindness and charity and logic can only be used for gold It shows how deeply money has corrupted the hearts of most men

Now, to get back to Dickie Loeb He was a child The books he read by day were not the books he read by night We are all of us moulded somewhat

The Loeb-Leopold Case

by the influences around us and, on people who read, perhaps books are the greatest and the strongest of these influences. We all know where our lives have been influenced by books. The nurse, strict and jealous and watchful, gave him one kind of books, by night he would steal off and read the other.

Which, think you, shaped the life of Dickie Loeb? Is there any kind of question about it? A child was it pure maliciousness? Was a boy of five or six or seven to blame for it? Where did he get it? He got it where we all get our ideas, and these books became a part of his dreams and a part of his life, and as he grew up his visions grew to hallucinations. He went out on the street and fantastically directed his companions, who were not there, in their various moves to complete the perfect crime.

Before I would tie a noose around the neck of a boy I would try to call back into my mind the emotions of youth. I would try to remember what the world looked like to me when I was a child. I would try to remember how strong were these instinctive, persistent emotions that moved my life. I would try to remember how weak and inefficient was youth in the presence of the surging, controlling feelings of the child. One that honestly remembers and asks himself the question and tries to unlock the door that he thinks is closed, and calls back the boy, can understand the boy.

But, your Honor, that is not all there is to boyhood. Nature is strong and she is pitiless. She works in her own mysterious way, and we are her victims. We have not much to do with it ourselves. Nature takes this job in hand, and we play our parts. In the words of old Omar Khayyam, we are only

> Impotent pieces in the game He plays
> Upon this checkerboard of nights and days
> Hither and thither moves, and checks, and slays,
> And one by one back in the closet lays

What had this boy to do with it? He was not his own father, he was not his own mother, he was not his own grandparents. All of this was handed to him. He did not surround himself with governesses and wealth. And yet he is to be compelled to pay.

There was a time in England, running down as late as the beginning of the last century, when judges used to convene court and call juries to try a horse, a dog, a pig, for crime. I have in my library a story of a judge and jury and lawyers trying and convicting an old sow for lying down on her ten pigs and killing them.

Do you mean to tell me that Dickie Loeb had any more to do with his making than any other product of heredity that is born upon the earth?

At this period of life it is not enough to take a boy — your Honor, I wish I knew when to stop talking about this question that always has interested me so much — it is not enough to take a boy filled with

The Loeb-Leopold Case

his dreams and his phantasies and living in an unreal world, but the age of adolescence comes on him with all the rest. What does he know? Both these boys are in the adolescent age, both these boys as every alienist in this case on both sides tells you, are in the most trying period of the life of a child, both these boys, when the call of sex is new and strange, both these boys at a time seeking to adjust their young lives to the world, moved by the strongest feelings and passions that have ever moved men; both these boys, at the time boys grow insane, at the time crimes are committed, all of this is added to all the rest of the vagaries of their lives. Shall we charge them with full responsibility that we may have a hanging? That we may deck Chicago in a holiday garb and let the people have their fill of blood, that you may put stains upon the heart of every man, woman and child on that day, and that the dead walls of Chicago will tell the story of the shedding of their blood?

For God's sake, are we crazy? In the face of history, of every line of philosophy, against the teaching of every religionist and seer and prophet the world has ever given us, we are still doing what our barbaric ancestors did when they came out of the caves and the woods.

From the age of fifteen to the age of twenty or twenty-one, the child has the burden of adolescence, of puberty and sex thrust upon him. Girls are kept at home and carefully watched. Boys without instruction are left to work the period out for themselves. It may lead to excess. It may lead to disgrace. It may lead to perversion. Who is to blame?

Your Honor, it is the easiest thing in the world to be a parent. We talk of motherhood, and yet every woman can be a mother. We talk of fatherhood, and yet every man can be a father. Nature takes care of that. It is easy to be a parent. But to be wise and farseeing enough to understand the boy is another thing, only a very few are so wise and so farseeing as that. When I think of the light way Nature has of picking out parents and populating the earth, having them born and die, I cannot hold human beings to the same degree of responsibility that young lawyers hold them when they are enthusiastic in a prosecution. I know what it means.

I know there are no better citizens in Chicago than the fathers of these poor boys. I know there were no better women than their mothers. But I am going to be honest with this court, if it is at the expense of both. I know that one of two things happened to Richard Loeb, that this terrible crime was inherent in his organism, and came from some ancestor, or that it came through his education and his training after he was born. Do I need to prove it? Judge Crowe said at one point in this case, when some witness spoke about their wealth that probably that was responsible.

To believe that any boy is responsible for himself or his early training is an absurdity that no lawyer or judge should be guilty of today. Somewhere this came to this boy. If his failing came from his heredity, I do not know where or how. None of us are bred perfect and pure, and the color of our hair, the color of our eyes, our stature, the weight and fineness of our brain, and everything about us could, with full knowledge, be traced with absolute certainty, if we had the pedigree it could be traced just the same in a boy as it could be in a dog, a horse, or cow.

I do not know what remote ancestors may have sent down the seed that corrupted him, and I do not know through how many ancestors it may have passed until it reached Dickie Loeb. All I know is that it is true, and there is not a biologist in the world who will not say that I am right. If it did not come that way, then I know that if he was normal, if he had been understood, if he had been trained as he should have been, it would not have happened. Not that anybody may not slip, but I know it and your Honor knows it, and every schoolhouse and every church in the land are evidences of it. Else why build them?

Every effort to protect society is an effort toward training the youth to keep the path. Every bit of training in the world proves it, and it likewise proves that it sometimes fails. I know that if this boy had been understood and properly trained — properly for him — and the training that he got might have been the very best for some one else —

but if it had been the proper training for him he would not be in this court room today with the noose above his head. If there is responsibility anywhere, it is back of him, somewhere in the infinite number of his ancestors or in his surroundings, or in both.

We may have all the dreams and visions and build all the castles we wish, but the castles of youth should be discarded with youth and when they linger to the time when boys should think wiser things, then it indicates a diseased mind. "When I was young I thought as a child, I spoke as a child, I understood as a child, but now I have put off childish things," said the Psalmist twenty centuries ago. It is when these dreams of boyhood, these phantasies of youth still linger, and the growing boy is still a child — a child in emotion, a child in feeling, a child in hallucinations — that you can say that it is the dreams and the hallucinations of childhood that are responsible for his conduct.

There is not an act in all this horrible tragedy that was not the act of a child, the act of a child wandering around in the morning of life, moved by the new feelings of a boy, moved by the uncontrolled impulses which his teaching was not strong enough to take care of, moved by the dreams and the hallucinations which haunt the brain of a child. I say, your Honor, that it would be the height of cruelty, of injustice, of wrong and barbarism to visit the penalty upon this boy.

Your Honor again I want to say that all parents can be criticized, likewise grandparents and teachers. Science is not so much interested in criticism as in finding causes. Sometime education will be more scientific. Sometime we will try to know the boy before we educate him and as we educate him. Sometime we will try to know what will fit the individual boy, instead of putting all boys through the same course, regardless of what they are.

This boy needed more of home, more love, more directing. He needed to have his emotions awakened. He needed guiding hands along the serious road that youth must travel. Had these been given him, he would not be here today.

Now, your Honor, I want to speak of the other lad, Babe. Babe is somewhat older than Dick, and is a boy of remarkable mind — away beyond his years. He is a sort of freak in this direction, as in others; a boy without emotions, a boy obsessed of philosophy, a boy obsessed of learning, busy every minute of his life.

He went through school quickly, he went to college young, he could learn faster than almost everybody else. His emotional life was lacking, as every alienist in this case excepting Dr. Krohn has told you. He was just a half boy, an intellect, an intellectual machine going without balance and without a governor, seeking to find out everything there was in life intellectually, seeking to solve every philosophy, but using his intellect only.

Of course his family did not understand him, few men would. His mother died when he was young, he had plenty of money, everything was given to him that he wanted. Both these boys with unlimited money, both these boys with automobiles, both of these boys with every luxury around them and in front of them. They grew up in this environment.

Babe took up philosophy. I call him Babe, not because I want it to affect your Honor, but because everybody else does. He is the youngest of the family and I suppose that is why he got his nickname. Mr. Crowe thinks it is easier to hang a man than a boy, and so I will call him a man if I can think of it. He grew up in this way. He became enamoured of the philosophy of Nietzsche.

Your Honor, I have read almost everything that Nietzsche ever wrote. He was a man of a wonderful intellect, the most original philosopher of the last century. A man who probably has made a deeper imprint on philosophy than any other man within a hundred years, whether right or wrong. More books have been written about him than probably all the rest of the philosophers in a hundred years. More college professors have talked about him. In a way he has reached more people, and still he has been a philosopher of what we might call the intellectual cult. Nietzsche believed that sometime the superman would be born; that evolution was working toward the superman.

He wrote one book, ' Beyond Good and Evil,"

The Loeb-Leopold Case

which was a criticism of all moral codes as the world understands them, a treatise holding that the intelligent man is beyond good and evil, that the laws for good and the laws for evil do not apply to those who approach the superman He wrote some ten or fifteen volumes on his various philosophical ideas Nathan Leopold is not the only boy who has read Nietzsche He may be the only one who was influenced in the way that he was influenced

I have just made a few short extracts from Nietzsche, that show the things that Nathan read and which no doubt influenced him These extracts are short and taken almost at random It is not how this would affect you It is not how it would affect me The question is, how it did affect the impressionable, visionary, dreamy mind of a boy?

At sixteen, at seventeen at eighteen, while healthy boys were playing baseball, or working on the farm, or doing odd jobs, he was reading Nietzsche, a boy who never should have seen it, at that early age Babe was obsessed of it, and here are some of the things which Nietzsche taught

> Why so soft, oh, my brethren? Why so soft, so unresisting and yielding? Why is there so much disavowal and abnegation in your heart? Why is there so little fate in your looks? For all creators are hard, and it must seem blessedness unto you to press your hand upon millenniums and upon wax This new table, oh, my brethren, I put over you Become hard To be obsessed by moral consideration presupposes a very low grade of intellect We should substitute for morality the will to

our own end, and consequently to the means to accomplish that

A great man, a man that nature has built up and invented in a grand style, is colder, harder, less cautious and more free from the fear of public opinion. He does not possess the virtues which are compatible with respectability, with being respected, nor any of those things which are counted among the virtues of the hard

Nietzsche held a contemptuous, scornful attitude to all those things which the young are taught as important in life, a fixing of new values which are not the values by which any normal child has ever yet been reared — a philosophical dream, containing more or less truth that was not meant by anyone to be applied to life

Counsel have said that because a man believes in murder that does not excuse him Quite right But this is not a case like the Anarchists Case, where a number of men, perhaps honestly believing in revolution and knowing the consequences of their act and knowing its illegal character, were held responsible for murder Of course the books are full of statements that the fact that a man believes in committing a crime does not excuse him

That is not this case, and counsel must know that it is not this case Here is a boy at sixteen or seventeen becoming obsessed with these doctrines There isn't any question about the facts Their own witnesses tell it and our witnesses tell it It was not a casual bit of philosophy with him, it was his life

He believed in a superman. He and Dickie Loeb were the supermen. There might have been others, but they were two, and two chums. The ordinary commands of society were not for him. Many of us read this philosophy but know that it has no actual application to life, but not he. It became a part of his being. He lived it and practiced it, he thought it applied to him, and he could not have believed it excepting that it either caused a diseased mind or was the result of a diseased mind.

In New York State a man named Freeman became obsessed in a very strange way of religious ideas. He read the story of Isaac and Abraham and he felt a call that he must sacrifice his son. He arranged an altar in his parlor. He converted his wife to the idea. He took his little babe and put it on the altar and cut its throat. Was he sane? Was he normal? Was this poor fellow responsible? Not in the least. And he was acquitted because he was the victim of a delusion. Men are largely what their ideas make them. Boys are largely what their ideas make them.

You remember that I asked Dr. Church about these religious cases and he said, " Yes, many people go to the insane asylum on account of them," that " they place a literal meaning on parables and believe them thoroughly." I asked Dr. Church, whom I again say I believe to be an honest man, and an intelligent man — I asked him whether the same thing might be done or might come from a philosophical belief, and he said, "If one believed it strongly enough."

And I asked him about Nietzsche. He said he knew something of Nietzsche, something of his responsibility for the war, for which he perhaps was not responsible. He said he knew something about his doctrines. I asked him what became of him, and he said he was insane for fifteen years just before the time of his death. His very doctrine is a species of insanity.

Here is a man a wise man — perhaps not wise, but brilliant — a thoughtful man who has made his impress upon the world. Every student of philosophy knows him. His own doctrines made him a maniac. And here is a young boy, in the adolescent age, harassed by everything that harasses children, who takes this philosophy and believes it literally.

Do you suppose this mad act could have been done by him in any other way? What could he have to win from this homicide? A boy with a beautiful home, with automobiles, a graduate of college, going to Europe, and then to study law at Harvard, as brilliant in intellect as any boy that you could find, a boy with every prospect that life might hold out to him, and yet he goes out and commits this strange, wild act, that he may die on the gallows or live in a prison cell until he dies of old age or disease. He did it, obsessed of an idea, perhaps to some extent influenced by what has not been developed publicly in this case — perversions that were present in the boy. All proving a diseased mind.

Now, I have said, that, as to Loeb if there is anybody to blame it is back of him. Your Honor, lots of things happen in this world that nobody is to blame for. In fact I am not very much for settling blame myself. If I could settle the blame on somebody else for this special act, I would wonder why that somebody else did it and I know if I could find that out I would move it back still another peg. I know, your Honor, that every atom of life in all this universe is bound up together. I know that a pebble cannot be thrown into the ocean without disturbing every drop of water in the sea. I know that every life is inextricably mixed and woven with every other life. I know that every influence, conscious and unconscious, acts and reacts on every living organism, and that no one can fix the blame. I know that all life is a series of infinite chances, which sometimes result one way and sometimes another. I have not the infinite wisdom that can fathom it, neither has any other human brain. But I do know that if back of it is a power that made it, that power alone can tell, and if there is no power, then it is an infinite chance, which man cannot solve.

Why should this boy's life be bound up with Frederick Nietzsche, who died, a few years ago, insane, in Germany? I don't know. I only know it is. I know that no man who ever wrote a line that I read failed to influence me to some extent. I know that every life I ever touched influenced me, and I influenced it, and that it is not given to me to unravel the infinite causes and say, " This is I, and this is you, I am responsible for so much, and you are responsible for so much." I know that in the universe everything has its place and that the smallest particle is a part of all. Tell me that you can visit the wrath of fate and chance and life and eternity upon a nineteen-year-old boy! If you could, justice would be a travesty and mercy a fraud.

I might say further about Nathan Leopold — where did he get this philosophy? At college? He did not make it, your Honor. He did not write these books, and I will venture to say there are at least ten thousand books on Nietzsche and his philosophy. There is no university in the world where the professors are not familiar with Nietzsche, not one. There is not an intellectual man in the world whose life and feelings run to philosophy, who is not more or less familiar with the Nietzschean philosophy. Some believe it, and some do not believe it. Some read it as I do and take it as a theory, a dream, a vision mixed with good and bad, but not in any way related to human life. Some take it seriously. The universities perhaps do not all teach it, for perhaps some teach nothing in philosophy but they give the boys the books of the masters, and tell them what they taught, and discuss the doctrines

I will guarantee that you can go down to the University of Chicago today — into its big library — and find over a thousand volumes on Nietzsche, and I am sure I speak moderately Your Honor, it is hardly fair to hang a nineteen-year-old boy for the philosophy that was taught him at the university The university, the scholars and publishers of the world would be more to blame than he is

Now, I do not want to be misunderstood about this Even for the sake of saving the lives of my clients, I do not want to be dishonest, and tell the court something that I do not honestly think in this case I do not believe that the universities are to blame I do not think they should be held responsible I do think, however, that they are too large, and that they should keep a closer watch, if possible, upon the individual But, you cannot destroy thought because, forsooth, some brain may be deranged by thought It is the duty of the university, as I conceive it, to be the great storehouse of the wisdom of the ages, and to let students go there, and learn, and choose I have no doubt that it has meant the death of many, that we cannot help Every changed idea in the world has had its consequences Every new religious doctrine has created its victims Every new philosophy has caused suffering and death. Every new machine has carved up men while it served the world No railroad can be built without the destruction of human life. No great building can be erected but that unfortunate workmen fall to the earth and die. No great movement that does not bear its toll of life and death, no great ideal but does good and harm, and we cannot stop because it may do harm.

I have no idea in this case that this act would ever have been committed or participated in by him excepting for the philosophy which he had taken literally, which belonged to older boys and older men, and which no one can take literally and practice literally and live. So, your Honor, I do not mean to unload this act on that man or this man, on this organization or that organization. I am trying to trace causes. I am trying to trace them honestly. I am trying to trace them with the light I have.

There is something else in this case, your Honor, that is stronger still. There is a large element of chance in life. I know I will die. I don't know when, I don't know how, I don't know where, and I don't want to know. I know it will come. I know that it depends on infinite chances. Do I live to myself? Did I make myself? And control my fate? Can I fix my death unless I suicide? I cannot do that because the will to live is too strong.

My death will depend upon chances. It may be by the taking in of a germ, it may be a pistol, it may be the decaying of my faculties, and all that makes life, it may be a cancer, it may be any one of an indefinite number of things, and where I am at a certain time, and whether I take in that germ, and the condition of my system when I breathe is an accident which is sealed up in the book of fate and which no human being can open

These boys, neither one of them, could have committed this act excepting by coming together. It was not the act for one, it was the act of two. It was the act of their planning, their conniving, their believing in each other, their thinking themselves supermen. Without it they could not have done it. It would not have happened. Their parents happened to meet, these boys happened to meet, some sort of chemical alchemy operated so that they cared for each other, and poor Bobby Franks' dead body, stripped and naked, was left in a culvert down near the Indiana line. I know it came through the mad act of mad boys. Mr. Savage told us that Franks, if he lived, would have been a great man. I want to leave this thought with your Honor now. I do not know what Bobby Franks would have been had he grown to be a man. I do not know the laws that control one's growth. Sometimes, your Honor, a boy of great promise is cut off in his early youth. Sometimes he dies and is placed in a culvert. Sometimes a boy of great promise stands on a trapdoor and is hanged by the neck until dead. Sometimes he dies of diphtheria. Death somehow pays no attention to age, sex, prospects, wealth or intellect.

It comes, and perhaps — I can only say perhaps, for I never professed to unravel the mysteries of fate, and I cannot tell — perhaps the boy who died at fourteen did as much as if he had died at seventy, and perhaps the boy who died as a babe did as much as if he had lived longer Perhaps, somewhere in fate and chance, it might be that he lived as long as he should

And I want to say this that the death of poor little Bobby Franks should not be in vain Would it mean anything if on account of that death, these two boys were taken out and a rope tied around their necks and they died felons? Would that show that Bobby Franks had a purpose in his life and a purpose in his death? No, your Honor, the unfortunate and tragic death of this weak young lad should mean something It should mean an appeal to the fathers and the mothers, an appeal to the teachers, to the religious guides, to society at large It should mean an appeal to all of them to appraise children, to understand the emotions that control them, to understand the ideas that possess them, to teach them to avoid the pitfalls of life

I have discussed somewhat in detail these two boys separately. Their coming together was the means of their undoing Your Honor is familiar with the facts in reference to their association They had a weird, almost impossible relationship Leopold, with his obsession of the superman, had repeatedly said that Loeb was his idea of the superman He had the attitude toward him that one has to his most devoted friend, or that a man has to a

The Loeb-Leopold Case

lover. Without the combination of these two, nothing of this sort probably could have happened It is not necessary for us, your Honor, to rely upon words to prove the condition of these boys' minds, and to prove the effect of this strange and fatal relationship between these two boys

It is mostly told in a letter which the State itself introduced in this case Not the whole story, but enough of it is shown, so that I take it that no intelligent, thoughtful person could fail to realize what was the relation between them and how they had played upon each other to effect their downfall and their ruin I want to read this letter, a letter dated October 9th, a month and three days before their trip to Ann Arbor, and I want the court to say in his own mind whether this letter was anything but the product of a diseased mind, and if it does not show a relationship that was responsible for this terrible homicide This was written by Leopold to Loeb They lived close together, only a few blocks from each other, saw each other every day, but Leopold wrote him this letter:

October 9, 1923.

Dear Dick

In view of our former relations, I take it for granted that it is unnecessary to make any excuse for writing you at this time, and still I am going to state my reasons for so doing, as this may turn out to be a long letter, and I don t want to cause you the inconvenience of reading it all to find out what it contains if you are not interested in the subjects dealt with

The Loeb-Leopold Case

First, I am enclosing the document which I mentioned to you today, and which I will explain later. Second, I am going to tell you of a new fact which has come up since our discussion. And third, I am going to put in writing what my attitude is toward our present relations, with a view of avoiding future possible misunderstandings, and in the hope (though I think it rather vain) that possibly we may have misunderstood each other, and can yet clear this matter up.

Now, as to the first, I wanted you this afternoon and still want you to feel that we are on an equal footing legally, and, therefore, I purposely committed the same tort of which you were guilty, the only difference being that in your case the facts would be harder to prove than in mine should I deny them. The enclosed document should secure you against changing my mind in admitting the facts if the matter should come up, as it would prove to any court that they were true.

As to the second. On your suggestion I immediately phoned Dick Rubel, and speaking from a paper prepared beforehand (to be sure of the exact wording) said "Dick when we were together yesterday did I tell you that Dick (Loeb) had told me the things which I then told you, or that it was merely my opinion that I believed them to be so?" I asked this twice to be sure he understood, and on the same answer both times (which I took down as he spoke) felt that he did understand. He replied 'No, you did not tell me that Dick told you these things, but said that they were in your opinion true."

He further denied telling you subsequently that I had said that they were gleaned from conversation with you, and I then told him that he was quite right, that you never had told me. I further told him that this was merely your suggestion of how to settle a question of fact, that he was in no way implicated, and that neither of us would be angry with him at his reply (I imply your assent to this) This of course proves that you were mistaken this afternoon in the question of my having actually and technically broken confidence and voids my apology, which I made contingent on proof of this matter

Now, as to the third, last, and most important question When you came to my home this afternoon I expected either to break friendship with you or attempt to kill you unless you told me why you acted as you did yesterday You did, however, tell me, and hence the question shifted to the fact that I would act as before if you persisted in thinking me treacherous, either in act (which you waived if Dick's opinion went with mine) or in intention

Now, I apprehend, though here I am not quite sure, that you said that you did not think me treacherous in intent, nor ever have, but that you considered me in the wrong and expected such a statement from me This statement I unconditionally refused to make until such time as I may become convinced of its truth

However, the question of our relation I think must be in your hands (unless the above conceptions are mistaken) inasmuch as you have satisfied first one and then the other requirement, upon which I agreed to refrain from attempting to kill you or refusing to continue our friendship Hence I have no reason not to continue to be on friendly terms with you, and would under ordinary conditions continue as before

The only question, then, is with you You demand me to perform an act, namely, state that I acted wrongly This I refuse Now it is up to you to inflict the penalty for this refusal — at your discretion, to break friendship, inflict physical punishment or anything else you like, or on the other hand to continue as before. The decision, therefore, must rest with you. This is all of my opinion on the right and wrong of the matter.

Now comes a practical question. I think that I would ordinarily be expected to, and in fact do expect to continue my attitude toward you as before until I learn either by direct words or by conduct on your part which way your decision has been formed. This I shall do.

Now a word of advice. I do not wish to influence your decision either way, but I do want to warn you that in case you deem it advisable to discontinue our friendship, that in both our interests extreme care must be had. The motif of "A falling out of ———" would be sure to be popular, which is patently undesirable and forms an irksome but unavoidable bond between us. Therefore, it is in my humble opinion, expedient though our breech need be no less real in fact, yet to observe the conventionalities, such as salutation on the street and a general appearance of at least not unfriendly relations on all occasions when we may be thrown together in public.

Now, Dick, I am going to make a request to which I have perhaps no right, and yet which I dare to make also for 'Auld Lang Syne. Will you, if not too inconvenient, let me know your answer (before I leave tomorrow) on the last count? This, to which I have no right, would greatly help my peace of mind in the next few days when it is most necessary to me. You can if you will merely call up my home before 12 noon and leave a message saying, ' Dick says yes," if you wish our relations to continue as before, and " Dick says no," if not.

It is unnecessary to add that your decision will of course have no effect on my keeping to myself our confidences of the past, and that I regret the whole affair more than I can say.

The Loeb-Leopold Case

Hoping not to have caused you too much trouble in reading this, I am (for the present) as ever,

BABE

Now, I undertake to say that under any interpretation of this case, taking into account all the things your Honor knows, that have not been made public, or leaving them out, nobody can interpret that letter excepting on the theory of a diseased mind, and with it goes this strange document which was referred to in the letter:

I, Nathan F. Leopold, Jr. being under no duress or compulsion, do hereby affirm and declare that on this, the 9th day of October, 1923, I for reasons of my own locked the door of the room in which I was with one Richard A. Loeb, with the intent of blocking his only feasible mode of egress, and that I further indicated my intention of applying physical force upon the person of the said Richard A. Loeb if necessary to carry out my design, to-wit, to block his only feasible mode of egress.

There is nothing in this case, whether heard alone by the court or heard in public, that can explain these documents, on the theory that the defendants were normal human beings.

The same may be said also of the other letter, dated October 10, from Babe if I may be permitted to call him Babe until you hang him.* If the expressions in those letters are sane expressions, your Honor, the rest of the world is crazy.

* EDITOR'S NOTE.— The letter here referred to by Mr. Darrow is printed in full beginning on page 222 of this volume.

The Loeb-Leopold Case

Now, both sides have called alienists and I will refer to that for a few moments. The facts here are plain, when these boys had made the confession on Sunday afternoon before their counsel or their friends had any chance to see them, Mr Crowe sent out for four men. He sent out for Dr Patrick, who is an alienist, Dr Church, who is an alienist; Dr Krohn, who is a witness, a testifier, and Dr Singer, who is pretty good — I would not criticize him but I would not class him with Patrick and with Church

I have said to your Honor that in my opinion he sent for the two ablest men in Chicago as far as the public knows them, Dr Church and Dr Patrick You heard Dr Church's testimony. Dr Church is an honest man though an alienist. He admitted the failure of emotional life in these boys, he admitted its importance he admitted the importance of beliefs strongly held in human conduct, he said himself that if he could get at all the facts he would understand what was back of this strange murder Every single position that we have claimed in this case Dr Church admitted

Dr Singer did the same. The only difference between them was this, it took but one question to get Dr Church to admit it, and it took ten to a dozen to get Dr Singer

Now, what did they do in their examination? What kind of a chance did these alienists have? It is perfectly obvious that they had none. Church, Patrick, Krohn went into a room with these two boys who had been in the possession of the State's Attorney's office for sixty hours, they were surrounded by policemen, were surrounded by guards and detectives and State's Attorneys, twelve or fifteen of them, and here they told their story. Of course this audience had a friendly attitude toward them. I know my friend Judge Crowe had a friendly attitude because I saw divers, various and sundry pictures of Prosecutor Crowe taken with these boys. When I first saw them I believed it showed friendship for the boys, but now I am inclined to think that he had them taken just as a lawyer who goes up in the country fishing has his picture taken with his catch.

The boys had been led doubtless to believe that these people were friends. They were taken there, in the presence of all this crowd. What was done? The boys told their story, and that was all.

Of course, Krohn remembered a lot that did not take place — and we would expect that of him, and he forgot much that did take place — and we would expect that of him, too. So far as the honest witnesses were concerned, they said that not a word was spoken excepting a little conversation upon birds, and the relation of the story that they had already given to the State's Attorney, and from that, and nothing else, both Patrick and Church said they showed no reaction as ordinary persons should show it, and intimated clearly that the commission of the crime itself would put them on inquiry as to

The Loeb-Leopold Case

whether these boys were mentally right, both admitted that the conditions surrounding them made the right kind of examination impossible, both admitted that they needed a better chance to form a reliable opinion. The most they said was that at this time they saw no evidence of insanity.

Singer did a thing more marvelous still. He never saw these boys until he came into this court excepting when they were brought down in violation of their constitutional rights to the office of Judge Crowe, after they had been turned over to the jailer, and there various questions were asked them, and to all of these the boys replied that they respectfully refused to answer on advice of counsel. And yet that was enough for Singer.

First of all we called Dr. William A. White. And who is he? For many years he has been superintendent of the Government Hospital for the Insane in Washington, a man who has written more books delivered more lectures and had more honors and knows this subject better than all their alienists put together, a man who knows his subject, and whose ability and truthfulness must have impressed this court.

Whom else did we get? Do I need to say anything about Dr. Healy? Is there any question about his integrity? A man who seldom goes into court except upon the order of the court. No man stands higher in Chicago than Dr. Healy. No man has done as much work in the study of adolescence

No man has read or written or thought or worked as much with the young No man knows the adolescent boy as well as Dr Healy Dr Healy began his research and his practice in Chicago and was the first psychiatrist of the boys' court He was then made a director of the Baker Foundation of Boston and is now carrying on his work in connection with the courts of Boston His books are known wherever men study boys His reputation is known all over the United States and in Europe

Dr Glueck, who was for years the alienist at Sing Sing and connected with the penal institutions in the State of New York, a man of eminent attainments and ripe scholarship

And Dr Hulbert, a young man who spent nineteen days in the examination of these boys, together with Dr Bowman an eminent doctor in his line from Boston These two physicians spent all this time getting every detail of these boys' lives, and structures, each one of these alienists took all the time needed for a thorough examination, without the presence of lawyers, detectives and policemen Each one of these psychiatrists tells this court the story, the sad, pitiful story, of the unfortunate minds of these two young lads

I submit, your Honor, that there can be no question about the relative value of these two sets of alienists, there can be no question that White, Glueck, Hulbert and Healy knew what they were talking about, for they had every chance to find out.

The Loeb-Leopold Case

They are either lying to this court, or their opinion is good. On the other hand, not one single man called by the State had any chance to know. He was called in to see these boys, the same as the State would call a hangman "Here are the boys, officer, do your duty." And that is all there was of it.

I want to discuss now another thing which this court must consider and which to my mind is absolutely conclusive in this case. That is, the age of these boys. I submit, your Honor, that it is not possible for any court to hang these two boys if he pays any attention whatever to the modern attitude toward the young, if he pays any attention whatever to the precedents in this country, if he pays any attention to the humane instincts which move ordinary men.

I have a list of executions in Cook County, beginning in 1840, which I presume covers the first one, because I asked to have it go to the beginning. Ninety poor unfortunate men have given up their lives to stop murder in Chicago. Ninety men have been hanged by the neck until dead, because of the ancient superstition that in some way hanging one keeps another from committing a crime. The ancient superstition, I say, because I defy the State to point to a criminologist, scientist, a student, who has ever said it. Still we go on, as if human conduct was not influenced and controlled by natural laws the same as all the rest of the universe is the subject of law. We treat crime as if it had no cause. We go on saying, "Hang the unfortunates, and it will end." Was there ever a murder without a cause? And yet all punishment proceeds upon the theory that there is no cause, and the only way to treat crime is to intimidate every one into goodness and obedience to law.

Crime has its cause. Perhaps all crimes do not have the same cause, but they all have some cause. And people today are seeking to find out the cause. Scientists are studying it, criminologists are investigating it, but we lawyers go on and on and on, punishing and hanging and thinking that by general terror we can stamp out crime.

If a doctor were called on to treat typhoid fever he would probably try to find out what kind of milk or water the patient drank, and perhaps clean out the well so that no one else could get typhoid from the same source. But if a lawyer were called on to treat a typhoid patient, he would give him thirty days in jail, and then he would think that nobody else would ever dare to take it. If the patient got well in fifteen days, he would be kept until his time was up; if the disease was worse at the end of thirty days, the patient would be released because his time was out. As a rule, lawyers are not scientists.

Still, we are making some progress. Courts give attention to some things that they did not give attention to before. Once in England they hanged children seven years of age, not necessarily hanged them, because hanging was never meant for punishment, it was meant for an exhibition If somebody committed a crime, he would be hanged by the head or the heels, it didn t matter much which, at the four crossroads, so that everybody could look at him until his bones were bare

Hanging was not necessarily meant for punishment The culprit might be killed in any other way, and then hanged — yes Hanging was an exhibition They were hanged on the highest hill, and hanged at the crossways, and hanged in public places, so that all men could see If there is any virtue in hanging. that was the logical way, because you cannot awe men into goodness unless they know about the hanging We have not grown better than the ancients We have grown more squeamish, we do not like to look at it, that is all They hanged them at seven years, they hanged them again at eleven and fourteen

We have raised the age of hanging We have raised it by the humanity of courts, by the understanding of courts, by the progress in science which at last is reaching the law, and of ninety men hanged in Illinois from its beginning, not one single person under twenty-three was ever hanged upon a plea of guilty — not one

First, I want to call your attention your Honor, to the cases on pleas of guilty in the State of Illinois Back of the year 1896 the record does not show ages After that, which is the large part, probably sixty out of ninety — all show the age Not the age at which they are hanged, but the age at the time of the verdict or sentence

The first hanging in Illinois — on a plea of guilty — was May 15, 1896, when a young colored man, 24 years old, was sentenced to death by Judge Baker

Judge Baker I knew very well; a man of ability, a fine fellow, but a man of moods I do not know whether the court remembers him, but that was the first hanging on a plea of guilty to the credit of any man in Illinois — I mean in Chicago I have not obtained the statistics from the rest of the State, but I am satisfied they are the same, and that boy was colored, and twenty-four, either one of which should have saved him from death, but the color probably had something to do with compassing his destruction

The next was Julius Mannow. Now, he really was not hanged on a plea of guilty, though the records so show I will state to your Honor just what the facts are Joseph Windreth and Julius Mannow were tried together in 1896 on a charge of murder with robbery When the trial was nearly finished Julius Mannow withdrew his plea of guilty He was defended by Elliott, whom I remember very well, and probably your Honor does And under what he supposed was an agreement with the court he plead this man guilty, after the case was nearly finished.

Now I am not here to discuss whether there was an agreement or not Judge Horton, who tried this

The Loeb-Leopold Case

case, did not sentence him but he waited for the jury's verdict on Windreth, and they found him guilty and sentenced him to death, and Judge Horton followed that sentence. Had this case come into that court on a plea of guilty, it probably would have been different. perhaps not, but it really was not a question of a plea of guilty, and he was twenty-eight or thirty years old

I might say in passing as to Judge Horton — he is dead. I knew him very well. In some ways I liked him. I tried a case for him after he had left the bench. But I will say this he was never noted in Chicago for his kindness and his mercy, and anybody who remembers knows that I am stating the truth

The next man who was hanged on a plea of guilty was Daniel McCarthy, twenty-nine years old, in 1897, by Judge Stein. Well, he is dead. I am very careful about being kind to the dead, so I will say that he never knew what mercy was, at least while he lived. Whether he does now, I cannot say. Still he was a good lawyer. That was in 1897

It was twenty-two years, your Honor, before anybody else was hanged in Cook County on a plea of guilty, old or young, twenty-two years before a judge had either the old or young walk into his court and throw himself on the mercy of the court and get the rope for it. But twenty-two years later, in 1919, Thomas Fitzgerald a man about forty years old, was sentenced for killing a little girl, plead guilty before my friend Judge Crowe, and he was put to death. And that is all. In the history of Cook County that is all that have been put to death on a plea of guilty. That is all.

Since that time one other man has been sentenced to death on a plea of guilty. That was James H. Smith, twenty-eight years old, sentenced by Judge Kavanagh. But we were spared his hanging. That was in January, 1923. I could tell you why he was sentenced to die. It was due to the cruelty that has paralyzed the hearts of men growing out of the war. We are accustomed to blood, your Honor. It used to look mussy, and make us feel squeamish. But we have not only seen it shed in buckets full, we have seen it shed in rivers, lakes and oceans, and we have delighted in it, we have preached it, we have worked for it, we have advised it, we have taught it to the young, encouraged the old, until the world has been drenched in blood, and it has left its stains upon every human heart and upon every human mind, and has almost stifled the feelings of pity and charity that have their natural home in the human breast.

I do not believe that Judge Kavanagh would ever have done this except for the great war which has left its mark on all of us, one of the terrible by-products of those wretched years. This man was reprieved, but James Smith was twenty-eight years old, he was old enough to vote, he was old enough to make contracts, he needed no guardian, he was old enough to do all the things that an older man can do. He was not a boy, a boy that is the special ward of the State, and the special ward of the court, and who cannot act except in special ways because he is not mature. He was twenty-eight and he is not dead and will not die. His life was saved, and you may go over every hanging, and if your Honor shall decorate the gallows with these two boys, your Honor will be the first in Chicago who has ever done such a deed. And I know you will not.

Your Honor, I must hasten along for I will close tonight. I know I should have closed before. Still there seems so much that I would like to say. I will spend a few more minutes on this record of hangings. There was one boy nineteen years old, Thomas Schultz, who was convicted by a jury and executed. There was one boy who has been referred to here, eighteen, Nicholas Viani, who was convicted by a jury and executed. No one else under twenty-one, your Honor, has been convicted by a jury and executed. Now, let me speak a word about these.

Schultz was convicted in 1912 and hanged. Of course, I believe it should not have happened, but your Honor knows the difference between a plea of guilty and a verdict. It is easy enough for a jury to divide the responsibility by twelve. They have not the charity which comes from age and experience. It is easy for some State's Attorneys to influence some juries. I don't know who defended the poor boy, but I guarantee that it was not the best lawyers at the bar, but doubtless a good lawyer prosecuted him, and when he was convicted the court said that he had rested his fate with the jury, and he would not disturb the verdict

I do not know whether your Honor, humane and considerate as I believe you to be, would have disturbed a jury's verdict in this case, but I know that no judge in Cook County ever himself upon a plea of guilty passed judgment of death in a case below the age of twenty-three, and only one at the age of twenty-three was ever hanged on a plea of guilty

Viani I have looked up, and I don't care who did it or how it was done, it was a shame and disgrace that an eighteen-year-old boy should be hanged, in 1920, or a nineteen-year-old boy should be hanged, in 1920, and I am assuming it is all right to hang somebody, which it is not

There were various things working against him. Most anything might have happened after the war, which I will speak of later, and not much later, for I am to close tonight There was a band of Italian desperadoes, so-called I don't know Sam Cardinelli was the leader, a man forty years of age But their records were very bad This boy should have been singled out from the rest. If I had been defending him, and he had not been, I never would have come into court again But he was not He was tried with the rest. I have looked up the records, and I find that he was in the position of most of these unfortunates, he did not have a lawyer.

Your Honor, the question of whether a man is convicted or acquitted does not always depend on the evidence or entirely on the judge or the jury. The lawyer has something to do with it. And the State always has — always has at least moderately good lawyers. And the defendants have, if they can get the money, and if they cannot, they have nobody. Ed Raber, if I am rightly informed, prosecuted. He had a fine chance, this poor Italian boy, tried with three or four others. And prosecuted by one of the most relentless prosecutors Chicago has ever known. This boy was defended by somebody whose name I never heard, who was appointed by the court.

Your Honor, if in this court a boy of eighteen and a boy of nineteen should be hanged on a plea of guilty, in violation of every precedent of the past, in violation of the policy of the law to take care of the young, in violation of the law that places boys in reformatories instead of prisons, if your Honor in violation of all that and in the face of all the past should stand here in Chicago alone to hang a boy on a plea of guilty, then we are turning our faces backward toward the barbarism which once possessed the world. If your Honor can hang a boy at eighteen, some other judge can hang him at seventeen, or sixteen, or fourteen Some day, if there is any such thing as progress in the world, if there is any spirit of humanity that is working in the hearts of men, some day men would look back upon this as a barbarous age which deliberately set itself in the way of progress, humanity and sympathy, and committed an unforgivable act

Yet your Honor has been asked to hang, and I must refer here for a minute to something which I dislike to discuss I hesitated whether to pass it by unnoticed or to speak of it, but feel that I must say something about it, and that was the testimony of Gortland, the policeman. He came into this court, the only witness who said that young Leopold told him that he might get into the hands of a friendly judge and succeed Your Honor, that is a blow below the belt There isn't a word of truth in his statement, as I can easily prove to your Honor It was carved out of the air, to awe and influence the court, and place him in a position where if he saved life some one might be malicious enough to say that he was a friendly judge, and, if he took it, the fear might invade the community that he did not dare to be merciful

Now, let me take Gortland's testimony for a minute He swore that on the night after the arrest of these two boys Nathan Leopold told him, in discussing the case, that a friendly judge might save him. He is the first man who testified for the State that any of us cross-examined, if you remember

They called witness after witness to prove something that did not need to be proved under a plea of guilty. Then this came, which to me was a poisoned piece of perjury, with a purpose, and I cross-examined him

"Did you make any record?" "Yes, I think I did."

"Where is it?" "I think I have it"

"Let me see it"

There was not a word or a syllable upon that paper

"Did you make any other?" "Yes"

"When did you make it?" "Within two or three days of the occurrence"

"Let me see that"

He said he would bring it back later

"Did you make another?" "Yes"

"What was it?" "A complete report to the chief of police"

"Is it in there?" "I think so"

"Will you bring that?" "Yes"

He brought them both into this court. They contained, all these reports, a complete or almost a complete copy of everything that happened, but not one word on this subject. He deliberately said that he made that record within a few days of the time it occurred, and that he told the office about it within a few days of the time it occurred. And then what did he say? Then he came back in answer to my cross-examination, and said that he never told

The Loeb-Leopold Case

Judge Crowe about it until the night before Judge Crowe made his opening statement in this case. Six weeks after he heard it, long after the time he said that he made a record of it, and there was not a single word or syllable about this matter in any report he made.

I am sorry to discuss it; I am sorry to embarrass this court, but what can I do? I want your Honor to know that if in your judgment you think these boys should hang, we will know it is your judgment. It is hard enough, for a court to sit where you sit, with the eyes of the world upon you, in the fierce heat of public opinion, for and against. It is hard enough, without any lawyer making it harder. I assure you it is with deep regret that I even mention the evidence, and I will say no more about it, excepting that this statement was deliberately false, and his own evidence shows it.

Now, your Honor, I have spoken about the war. I believed in it. I don't know whether I was crazy or not. Sometimes I think perhaps I was. I joined in the general cry. I urged men to fight. I was safe because I was too old to go. For four long years the civilized world was engaged in killing men. Christian against Christian, barbarians uniting with Christians to kill Christians, anything to kill. It was taught in every school, aye in the Sunday schools. The little children played at war. Do you suppose this world has ever been the same since then? How long, your Honor, will it take for the world to get back the humane emotions that were slowly growing before the war? We read of killing one hundred thousand men in a day. We read about it and we rejoiced in it — if it was the other fellows who were killed. We were fed on flesh and drank blood. Even down to the prattling babe. I need not tell your Honor this, because you know, I need not tell you how many upright, honorable young boys have come into this court charged with murder, boys who fought in this war and learned to place a cheap value on human life. You know it and I know it. These boys were brought up in it. The tales of death were in their homes, their playgrounds, their schools, they were in the newspapers that they read, it was a part of the common frenzy — what was a life? It was nothing. It was the least sacred thing in existence and these boys were trained to this cruelty.

It will take fifty years to wipe it out of the human heart, if ever. No one needs to tell me that crime has no cause. It has as definite a cause as any other disease, and I know that out of the hatred and bitterness of the Civil War crime increased as America had never known it before. I know that growing out of the Napoleonic wars there was an era of crime such as Europe had never seen before. I know that Europe is going through the same experience today, I know it has followed every war, and I know it has influenced these boys so that life was not the same to them as it would have been if the world had not been made red with blood. I protest against visiting upon them the crimes and mistakes of society. All of us have our share in it. I have mine. I cannot tell and I shall never know how many words of mine might have given birth to cruelty in place of love and kindness and charity.

Your Honor knows that in this very court crimes of violence have increased growing out of the war. Not necessarily by those who fought but by those that learned that blood was cheap, and human life was cheap, and if the State could take it lightly why not the boy? There are causes for this terrible crime. There are causes, as I have said, for everything that happens in the world. War is a part of it, education is a part of it, birth is a part of it, money is a part of it — all these conspired to compass the destruction of these boys.

Has the court any right to consider anything but these two boys? The State says that your Honor has a right to consider the welfare of the community, as you have. If the welfare of the community would be benefited by taking these lives, well and good. I think it would work evil that no one could measure. Has your Honor a right to consider the families of these two defendants? I have been sorry, and I am sorry for the bereavement of Mr. and Mrs. Franks, for those broken ties that cannot be healed. All I can hope and wish is that some good may come from it all. But as compared with the families of Leopold and Loeb, the Franks are to be envied — and everyone knows it

I do not know how much salvage there is in these two boys. I hate to say it in their presence, but what is there to look forward to? I do not know but what your Honor would be merciful if you tied a rope around their necks and let them die; merciful to them, but not merciful to civilization, and not merciful to those who would be left behind. To spend the balance of their days in prison is mighty little to look forward to, if anything. Is it anything? They may have the hope that as the years roll around they might be released. I do not know. I do not know. I will be honest with this court as I have tried to be from the beginning. I know that these boys are not fit to be at large. I believe they will not be until they pass through the next stage of life, at forty-five or fifty. Whether they will be then, I cannot tell. I am sure of this. I will not be here to help them. So far as I am concerned, it is over.

I would not tell this court that I do not hope that some time when life, age, has changed their bodies, as it does, and has changed their emotions, as it does, that they may once more return to life. I would be the last person on earth to close the door of hope to any human being that lives, and least of all to my clients. But what have they to look forward to? Nothing. And I think here of the stanza of Housman:

The Loeb-Leopold Case

> Now hollow fires burn out to black,
>   And lights are fluttering low
> Square your shoulders, lift your pack
>   And leave your friends and go
> O never fear, lads, naught's to dread,
>   Look not left nor right
> In all the endless road you tread
>   There's nothing but the night

I care not, your Honor, whether the march begins at the gallows or when the gates of Joliet close upon them, there is nothing but the night, and that is little for any human being to expect.

But there are others to consider. Here are these two families, who have led honest lives, who will bear the name that they bear, and future generations must carry it on.

Here is Leopold's father — and this boy was the pride of his life. He watched him, he cared for him, he worked for him, the boy was brilliant and accomplished, he educated him, and he thought that fame and position awaited him, as it should have. It is a hard thing for a father to see his life's hopes crumble into dust.

Should he be considered? Should his brothers be considered? Will it do society any good or make your life safer, or any human being's life safer, if it should be handed down from generation to generation, that this boy, their kin, died upon the scaffold?

And Loeb's the same. Here are the faithful uncle

The Loeb-Leopold Case

and brother, who have watched here day by day, while Dickie's father and his mother are too ill to stand this terrific strain, and shall be waiting for a message which means more to them than it can mean to you or me. Shall these be taken into account in this general bereavement? Have they any rights? Is there any reason, your Honor, why their proud names and all the future generations that bear them shall have this bar sinister written across them? How many boys and girls, how many unborn children will feel it? It is bad enough as it is, God knows. It is bad enough, however it is. But it's not yet death on the scaffold. It's not that. And I ask your Honor, to save two honorable families from a disgrace that never ends, and which could be of no avail to help any human being that lives.

Now, I must say a word more and then I will leave this with you where I should have left it long ago. None of us are unmindful of the public, courts are not, and juries are not. We placed our fate in the hands of a trained court, thinking that he would be more mindful and considerate than a jury. I cannot say how people feel. I have stood here for three months as one might stand at the ocean trying to sweep back the tide. I hope the seas are subsiding and the wind is falling, and I believe they are, but I wish to make no false pretense to this court. The easy thing and the popular thing to do is to hang my clients. I know it. Men

The Loeb-Leopold Case

and women who do not think will applaud The cruel and thoughtless will approve It will be easy today, but in Chicago, and reaching out over the length and breadth of the land more and more fathers and mothers, the humane, the kind and the hopeful, who are gaining an understanding and asking questions not only about these poor boys, but about their own — these will join in no acclaim at the death of my clients These would ask that the shedding of blood be stopped, and that the normal feelings of man resume their sway And as the days and the months and the years go on, they will ask it more and more

But, your Honor, what they shall ask may not count. I know the easy way I know your Honor stands between the future and the past I know the future is with me, and what I stand for here, not merely for the lives of these two unfortunate lads, but for all boys and all girls, for all of the young, and as far as possible, for all of the old I am pleading for life, understanding, charity, kindness, and the infinite mercy that considers all I am pleading that we overcome cruelty with kindness and hatred with love I know the future is on my side You may hang these boys; you may hang them by the neck until they are dead. But in doing it you will turn your face toward the past In doing it you are making it harder for every other boy who in ignorance and darkness must grope his way through the mazes which only childhood knows In doing it you will make it harder for unborn children You may save them and make it easier for every child that sometime may stand where these boys stand You will make it easier for every human being with an aspiration and a vision and a hope and a fate I am pleading for the future, I am pleading for a time when hatred and cruelty will not control the hearts of men When we can learn by reason and judgment and understanding and faith that all life is worth saving, and that mercy is the highest attribute of man

I feel that I should apologize for the length of time I have taken This case may not be as important as I think it is, and I am sure I do not need to tell this court, or to tell my friends, that I would fight just as hard for the poor as for the rich If I should succeed in saving these boys' lives and do nothing for the progress of the law, I should feel sad, indeed If I can succeed, my greatest reward and my greatest hope will be that I have done something for the tens of thousands of other boys, for the countless unfortunates who must tread the same road in blind childhood that these poor boys have trod — that I have done something to help human understanding, to temper justice with mercy, to overcome hate with love

I was reading last night of the aspiration of the old Persian poet, Omar Khayyam It appealed to me as the highest that I can vision I wish it were in my heart, and I wish it were in the hearts of all.

The Loeb-Leopold Case

> So I be written in the Book of Love,
> I do not care about that Book above
> Erase my name or write it as you will,
> So I be written in the Book of Love

Speech of Benjamin C Bachrach

MAY IT PLEASE YOUR HONOR AND YOU GENTLEMEN FOR THE PROSECUTION

WE are approaching the close of this momentous hearing, and as I address myself to your Honor, I have a feeling of humility and unworthiness

Mr Darrow has talked at length on the one subject, if your Honor please, that has troubled us here, that is a subject of discussion throughout the entire world What shall the punishment be? Shall it be death, or life imprisonment?

And, if your Honor please, on the subject of punishment, the subject that possesses your Honor's entire interest, you have been listening to a master He has told you, from his reading and study, of the growth and development of the ideas of punishment, from the ancient and barbarous past Your Honor remembers his speaking of a case in which they burned a girl thirteen years of age Here are six lines from Lawyers' Reports Annotated, mentioning this case I read from page 200

The case of the girl mentioned was that of Alice DeWalborough, who Hale tells us (1 Hale, Pleas, The

Crown, page 26) was burned to judgment when but thirteen years of age for the killing of her mistress, because by the ancient law none shall be hanged within age, which is intended the age of discretion namely, fourteen years.

The law could not hang her on account of her age, and so it burned her.

My friend, Mr Marshall, in the progress of this trial has read many court decisions — none in point They must have been collected to read to a jury before whom he expected to try this case But he had them here and read them on objections to evidence, motions to exclude evidence

He contended that your Honor had no right to hear anything in mitigation, but should only hear matters of aggravation, and having heard them in aggravation, the mitigation was wiped out, therefore, you have a simple, complete case which would fit a hanging punishment A wonderful plan of procedure, indeed

Now, let me show you something Mr Marshall read from Haensel, an Illinois case, 293 He pointed that out as a case which should convince your Honor that there is no merit in our position that the defendants at the bar should not be executed

The plaintiff in error met his wife, stuck a gun against her chest, demanded some papers, struck his mother-in-law in the head with a pair of pliers, and as she ran back in the bedroom fired a shot, which passed through the right side of her chest

He followed her, a number of shots were fired, and it was an insanity defense, the man was convicted, and so forth. Mr Marshall makes the comment that this man was in bad shape. He had syphilis, goiter, vertigo, and had been struck in the head. He had army service. There was some excuse for him. He was a sick man on all the showing made.

And then he goes on "There were no phantasies, there were no delusions, there were no hallucinations, but something of substance."

And after being here four weeks! How could he help you? What is the use? It can make no impression on him. Are delusions not matters of substance as far as mentality is concerned? Isn't that the last? Doesn't it mean anything to him?

Undoubtedly what he says is the foreword of what is going to be said by the State's Attorney. He will say it is all piffle. Teddy bears, phantasies, we all have phantasies, everybody has phantasies, even Dr Patrick. "I had phantasies," he said.

In this case we were not worried about Dr Patrick's phantasies. Dr Patrick is beyond the adolescent period, the period of puberty. I don't know what his phantasies were then, but the kind of phantasies he has now, getting along as well as he does, won't do him any harm.

Considerable has been said, your Honor, about the inability of the State's alienists to come to a just conclusion from their examination. It is claimed they made an examination. To repeat what has been said, Dr Krohn is the only one that was well satisfied with the conditions under which that examination was made

Your Honor will remember that the most loquacious of the psychiatrists for the State was Dr Krohn You remember my asking him as to dealing with each of the boys I call them boys, your Honor, for they are below twenty-one years of age I do not call them boys to deceive your Honor Your Honor knows just how old they are, how old or how young they look

I asked Krohn questions as to what he discovered in that examination He said, first the senses were all right, the logical reasoning was all right, the logical sequence was all right, there was a flowing stream of thought, a continuity of thought, and a perfect orientation as to time, place and social relations It sounds all right, intelligent, and looks as if we were getting somewhere But it appears, then, that all of those things are positively consistent with a psychopathic personality

When he found those things there, he had not been shown any evidence of mental disease Neither had any of the other psychiatrists

And at six-thirty o'clock, may it please your Honor, on Sunday, June 1st, if I may talk figuratively, the clerk of the court called mental disease three times in stentorian tones, and a forfeiture was declared They had not shown the alienists of the State that they had mental disease Of course, they did not try. Their souls were stripped bare, so they say, but because they did not show them, that was their conclusion, and they worded it carefully.

Dr. Patrick was the first one. He said, "There was no evidence of mental disease." He meant of course that he saw none, that none had been shown him.

Now, what was that examination? I won't go into a discussion as to whether my friend Judge Crowe feared the boys had a mental disease — and I want to say now lest I forget it, that I never saw a case of this importance so well prepared, and where the work was so expeditiously done as was done by Judge Crowe in this case.

It may be that he feared that the lawyers who might be thereafter retained would come into the court room with the only defense that he thought was possible, and that he was going to forestall them. Maybe he thought that there was no possibility of their being mentally diseased. Maybe he was in good faith on that, and thought all that was necessary to determine this case was to bring in some good alienists and say "Look them over, doctors. Are you through now? Did you look? Wait, I will have them tell the story about the murder, tell it in all the details. Now, you take notes, Leopold, and when he gets through you correct him on that."

The story goes along and then "What do you say?" Krohn tells the reporters "Sane." Krohn knew what was expected of him His response was adequate

Now, you have heard a good deal of criticism of that examination I have no desire to overdo it I want to bring up the point, what should they have done? Were they trying to find out only if the senses were alert, if the logic was good, if the continuity of thought was perfect, if the stream ran along, and if the accused boys knew where they were? Is that enough? Is that the way they find out whether men are insane or not?

How many people in this room are there that couldn't have determined the same identical things in this case that those four alienists determined on that day? The defendants have senses working They can hear They look at a book They read it correctly They talk They move around the room They don't seem to have their feet clogged up Their logic is good They argue with one another Why, the ordinary person would say, " Yes, they look to be sane, they look to be normal "

Of course they did They looked that way to their parents, to their brothers How do we know they looked that way? Mr Crowe knows they looked that way He knows that the father of Leopold, the uncle of Loeb, and the brother came down to see them when they were under investigation and they told him they felt it their duty to co-operate with him in every way They never dreamed what the truth of this case was

The Loeb-Leopold Case

Dr. White points out that when the child is born there is very little intelligence, but the emotions are working The child is hungry. A noise affects it It has a feeling of discomfort, warmth or cold, which it expresses by cries There is a reaction The child in its primitive emotion takes the food that is given it The child is not concerned with determining who pays for that food, whether it is honestly come by or not, whether the person who got it committed crimes for it The intelligence grows, and the emotional side grows, and at an early period of life impressions are given to the child

But if it does not happen, your Honor, that the emotional side of the child grows in parallel lines with the intellectual side, there will be the same difficulty in the mind of the child as there would be in the physical body if one arm grew regularly and the other was only half length In that case it would be a physical cripple, and the child with a mind that did not grow along parallel lines, on the intellectual side and the emotional side, would be an intellectual cripple

Now, I am not going to discuss the crime itself That has been done by Mr. Darrow But, having that in mind, knowing that much of the thing, the alienist talks to the boy or man, whoever it is, having a clue of that departure from the pattern, and finds out if the thing was an adequate emotional response to a given logical stimulus If it had been a crime of revenge, or passion, or something of that

The Loeb-Leopold Case

kind, it would be easy to understand But when you cannot find in the crime itself anything indicating what ordinary, normal people would understand as a sane reason, then you have a right to suspect that there is something wrong But it is not conclusive yet

Then they begin to examine, and, as they did in this case, they get the man to talk about his likes and his dislikes, his aims, his ambitions, his child life, his dreams, night dreams and daydreams, and the good doctor, and all of them told you, that the phantasies or daydreams were the things that the child had which compensated him for his disappointments in his daily facing the situations in life

They compensated him How? Because if he was normal he would have daydreams that would express his wish fulfillment, and they would be things that would be present to him along natural, normal lines

If there was a discrepancy between the emotional life and his intellectual life you might find in those phantasies a clue, and if you found morbid phantasies, diseased phantasies, and if you further found that they persisted for a long, long time and finally were projected into reality, you would begin to get on warm stuff

But it may be said in reply that these things could be invented, the phantasies, their operation, their application Fortunately, if your Honor please, as to the phantasies of Dickie Loeb, you received evidence of them from the State's Attorney before any designing person could have had the slightest opportunity of talking with him. As to the delusions of Leopold as a superman, and of Dickie Loeb as a superman we get evidence that dates back long prior to the commission of the crime

Your Honor will remember, if it is necessary to recall it, that when the argument occurred in the office of the State's Attorney on that notable Sunday of June 1, 1924, an argument between Dick Loeb and Babe Leopold — that is what the State's Attorney was calling them — in which Leopold tried to convince the State's Attorney that it was Loeb who struck the blows with the chisel and sat in the rear seat of the car, in order to prove it, he called attention to the fact that Richard Loeb was reading detective stories, playing detective, and had notions of being a criminal, a Master Criminal and so forth

Your Honor will remember the letter dated October 9 from Leopold to Loeb On the next day, after receiving a reply to this letter, Leopold again wrote to Loeb as follows

October 10, 20th Century Limited, 1 45 P M

Dear Dick I want to thank you first of all for your kindness in granting my request of yesterday I was highly gratified to hear from you for two reasons, the first sentimental and the second practical The first of these is that your prompt reply conclusively proved my previous idea that the whole matter really did mean something to you, and that you respected my wishes, even though we were not very friendly This is a great satisfaction but the second is even greater, in that I imply from the general tenor of your letter that there is a good chance of a reconciliation between us, which I ardently desire, and this belief will give me that peace of mind on which I based my request

But I fear, Dick, that your letter has failed to settle the controversy itself, as two points are still left open These I will not attack As I wrote you yesterday, the decision of our relations was in your hands, because it depended entirely on how you wished to treat my refusal to admit that I acted wrongly This request you do not answer You imply merely that because of my statement that 'I regret the whole matter' I am in part at least admitting what you desire I thought twice before putting that phrase in my letter, for fear you might misconstrue it, as in fact you have done First you will note that I said that 'I regret the whole matter' (not any single part of it) By this I meant that I regretted the crime you originally committed (your mistake in judgment) from which the whole consequences flow But I did not mean and do not wish to be understood as meaning that once this act had been done, I regret anything subsequent I do not in fact regret it, because I feel sure, as I felt from the beginning, that should we again become friends, it will be on a basis of better mutual understanding as deliberately planned and precipitated Further, even if I did regret those consequences, it would not follow at all that I consider myself to have acted wrongly I may regret that it is necessary to go downtown to the dentist, and still not feel that I am acting wrongly in so doing Quite the contrary. So if you insist on my stating that I acted wrongly, as a prerequisite to our renewal of friendship, I feel in duty bound to point out to you that this is not the meaning of what I wrote In this do not think that I am trying to avoid a renewal of these relations You know how much I desire a renewal but I still feel that I must point this out to you, as I could not consider re-entering those relations when you were under the misapprehension that I had conceded to what you demanded On the basis of this construction of my words, then, Dick, should you base your decision Next comes the other point of issue, namely, whether I wish to be a party to a reconciliation, supposing that you wish on the basis of the previous statements to do so Here the decision rests not with you, but with me Now, as I wrote you yesterday, you obviated my first reason for a refusal by telling me what I wanted to know, but another arose, the question of treachery, and that is not quite settled in my mind For the purpose of this discussion, I shall not use the short term 'treachery' as you suggested in your letter, to cover whatever you want to call it I have no desire to quibble over terms, and am sure we both mean the same thing as treachery Very well The whole question must be divided into two, namely, treachery in act and treachery in intention On your suggestion, the first was to be settled by phoning Dick, as I did, I apologizing verbally on condition that you were right, and implying the same apology from you in case you were wrong

You were proved wrong, and I am sure you are a good enough sport to stick by your statement, unless you question whether I did all you suggested in good faith Hence, you remove any previous charge of treachery in act If there was such But the second is not so simple I stated, and still hold, that if you still held me to have acted treacherously in intent, our friendship must cease You circumvent that by saying you never could have held this opinion because you believe me to have acted hastily, etc I did my best in stating that I was wholly responsible for all I said and did, since I had planned it all, and if there were malice at all it would be malice aforethought You refuse to believe me Now, that is not my fault I have done my best to tell you the true facts, (since they were in my disadvantage) and hence have discharged my obligation I still insist that I have planned all I did You can believe this or not as you like or come to your own decision, on whether you still think I acted treacherously If you say you do not, then I shall infer either that you never thought so (although you accuse me of it) or that you have changed your mind (and imply these as an apology for ever thinking so) and continue to be your friend All I want from you then is a statement that you do not now think me to have acted treacherously in intent, which I will construe as above Then it is up to you whether you will forego my statement of wrong action or will on your part break up our friendship Please wire me at my expense to the Biltmore Hotel, New York, immediately on receipt, stating, one, whether you wish to break our friendship or to forego my statement or, two, whether or not you still think me to have acted treacherously If you want further discussion on either point merely wire me that you must see me to discuss it before you decide Now, that is all that is in point to our controversy but I am going to add a little more in an effort to explain my system of a Nietzschian philosophy with regard to you It may not have occurred to you why a mere mistake in judgment on your part should be treated as a crime, when on the part of another it should not be so considered Here are the reasons In formulating a superman he is, on account of certain superior qualities inherent in him, exempted from the ordinary laws which govern ordinary men. He is not liable for anything he may do, whereas others would be, except for the one crime that it is possible for him to commit — to make a mistake.

Now, obviously any code which conferred upon an individual or upon a group extraordinary privileges without also putting on him extraordinary responsibility, would be unfair and bad. Therefore, an *uebermensch* is held to have committed a crime every time he errs in judgment — a mistake excusable in others. But you may say that you have previously made mistakes which I did not treat as crimes. This is true. To cite an example, the other night you expressed the opinion and insisted that Marcus Aurelius Antonius was, 'practically the founder of Stoicism,' and in so doing you committed a crime. But it was a slight crime and I chose to forgive it. Similarly I have, and had before this matter reached the present stage, forgiven the crime which you committed in committing the error in judgment which caused the whole train of events. I did not and do not wish to charge you with a crime, but I feel justified in using any of the consequences of your crime for which you were held responsible to my advantage. This and only this I did, so you see how careful you must be.

Now, Dick, just one more word to sum up. Supposing you fulfill both conditions necessary for our reconciliation. One, waive claim to my statement, and, two, state yourself that you no longer think me to have acted treacherously. We are going to be as good or better friends as before. I wanted that to come about very much, but not at the expense of your thinking that I have backed down in any way from my stand, as I am sure of that in my mind and want you to be

The Loeb-Leopold Case

Well Dick, the best of luck if I do not see you again and thanks in advance for the wire, I am sure you will be good enough to send Hoping you will be able to decide in the way I obviously want,

I am,
BABE

It was not fabricated for this case, was it? It was long before this happened Can any one come to the conclusion that that letter came from a normal mind?

I have indicated, your Honor, what the examination of the alienists for the State brought forth, and it was the senses, the logical sequence, orientation, the stream of thought and continuity of thought That is the best, the most positive statement that came from the alienists for the State

Now, the alienists for the defense I will just touch lightly on these things, your Honor will remember them Take Dickie Loeb first First they found an abnormal phantasy life The substance of the phantasies was peculiar, it was the phantasy of the commission of a perfect crime and about being abused in jail The next one was the prolongation into adolescence of these infantile phantasies They learned that

They learned also that he projected into the world of reality his phantasy life by endeavoring to conform conduct thereto, such as playing detective, playing gang leader, playing committing burglary as well as the actual commission of many crimes of a more or less serious nature. He also projected the phantasy into the world of reality in the ride in the police car. He told the reporters on that occasion that he always wanted to ride in a Marmon, and this was his opportunity. Of course the Marmon meant the police car. He lived out his phantasies by his life in the jail, his satisfaction in the jail life and his evident happiness that was described by all the alienists for the defense. That is one thing, all these things I put under one.

Now, they also discovered his criminalistic tendencies, or activity, the lying and boastfulness, the fainting spells, his infantile and twisted emotional development, making possible a consideration of his own brother and father as possible victims of kidnaping. His pathological desire for sympathy, his pathological desire for power. All these things a real examination disclosed.

More. The commission of crimes in order to have the feeling of superior knowledge over every one — you will remember that in the evidence — and mixing with a crowd to enjoy their evident confusion and ignorance.

The interest in the palpitation of his heart. His heart beat faster when he was engaged in some criminalistic enterprise.

He had an inferiority feeling. From early boyhood he had no opportunity to adjust himself and his emotions to real life.

The Loeb-Leopold Case

Now, this sudden precipitation of Dickie Loeb from early sheltered boyhood into college life, with the influence of older companions leading to drink and sex temptations that they learned, that is important, too. They get all their materials together and then they form a conclusion.

The influence of the nurse you have heard about. The heightened feeling of inferiority causing resort to crime as a method of a compensatory feeling of power, you are familiar with that. Also the pathological need for "showing off" before his associates in iniquity, and his admitted inability to commit crime without a companion before whom to demonstrate his superiority.

Then we come to the endocrine disorders, and then we come to Loeb's basal metabolism, seventeen per cent minus, and the instability of the nervous system. We find the disparity between his intellectual precocity and his emotional retardation, which was one of the things that the psychiatrists were looking for. Then they found his conduct in connection with the crime itself, absence of remorse, absence of disgust, absence of sympathy, absence of repulsion. They found his reaction to Mrs Franks' testimony, his reaction to the suggestion of murdering Walter Bachrach. They found his normal and customary behavior after the murder, the return to routine existence after the murder and before apprehension. He went along in life as usual, there was no difficulty about that, they took all that into consideration. They observed his actions and attitudes in the court room.

The alienists for the State observed them, too. They saw that he walked all right, that he smiled a good bit, and when Mr. Crowe raised some kind of a rumpus, and called attention to his constant smiling, he changed it. The others did not notice that he changed it at all. They smile once in a while, and they do not smile, just depending on how they feel.

Then they learned from that examination the thoughts and plans of suicide. They learned of the thoughts of killing Babe and Dick Rubel, and they saw from their experienced investigation a lack of judgment. This we found corroborated by witnesses who were called by the defense.

They found that he was willing to die, that he considered life complete, but that if he must go to jail for life, he would be satisfied if he could obtain a complete newspaper file dealing with the crime and the trial. So much they found out from Loeb.

I will go rapidly now, with reference to Leopold. They found out something about Leopold, his sex life, his early sex life. He had some trouble. There was a governess there. She was not there as long as the other. There were endocrine disorders. There was a phantasy life. There was the king-slave phantasy. There was a prolongation of the same phantasy over a period of years.

There was a projection of phantasies into the world at large, by the search for a superman whose will should govern his activities He found him eventually in Loeb

There was the hedonistic philosophy, and the superman idea He had a delusion that Dick measured up to the test of the superman, a delusion that was serious His letter of October 10, 1923, just read to your Honor, shows that You heard the statements of the witnesses called by the defense He talked superman to them He argued in the law class that the rules of law as to torts and crimes did not apply to him He said superman, but of course we all know he meant himself

Then we find that early in life he began a deliberate, intentional destruction of his emotional life He showed a willingness to kidnap his own father

He was conscious of setting out to lead a purely intellectual life, going to leave emotions out of it He used his intellectual precocity as a weapon with which to combat physical inferiority His interest in religion Your Honor remembers the churches The idea his mother was a Madonna his aunt was a Madonna He classified the churches His Christ idea His atheism That was confirmed by his mother's death And then came the tremendous disparity between his intellectual precocity and the appropriateness and adequacy of his emotional responses

His idea of grandeur and comparison of himself

in jail to Napoleon at St Helena His illnesses at puberty His lack of resistance to infection as disclosed by the examination

His feelings of inferiority His small stature. His attendance at the girls' school, being accompanied to the school by a nurse for many years His projection into college life at an early age, with the same temptations for drink and sex and the need of living up to the standards of much older men

His attitude towards hanging His readiness, his desire to show consistency His desire to leave puzzles for the scientists His desire to write an apologia His obvious lack of good judgment, which was even apparent to his companions who testified as lay witnesses His willingness to subject himself entirely to the hazards of a criminal career in order to obtain satisfaction of his pathological needs

He had a paranoid personality Loeb had a schizophrenic personality All these things were found during a real examination by our psychiatrists

There is no doubt he considered himself a superman If that was not a delusion and there was that in him which justified him in thinking he was a superman through normal tests, what do you think about what he did to that superman? Here was a superman in his custody He ruined the superman by this crime

Just one word more, if your Honor please, and I

am through. Here is the State urging that your Honor shall put these two boys to death. When the State's Attorney prepared his case and presented it to the Grand Jury and presented the matters in aggravation to your Honor he could have very appropriately and honorably stopped, without urging that there should be a maximum sentence. But he won't. He will go on and urge that your Honor ought to hang.

You are listening for the last time in this case to anybody on the part of the defense, humbly, may it please your Honor, frankly begging and pleading that you let the defendants live and not bring upon their families the great anxiety, bitterness and suffering that their deaths upon the gallows would bring.

I thank your Honor for your patience.

Speech of Robert E. Crowe

May it Please Your Honor

BEFORE entering into a discussion of the case at bar I desire to express our appreciation for the uniform courtesy and patience with which your Honor has treated me and the representatives of my office.

Our conduct in this case has been criticised by the defense. We ought not to refer to two murderers who have pleaded guilty to two capital offenses

as criminals, nor to their crimes as cold-blooded
We have violated the finer sensibilities of their
counsel

These two college graduates — the poor sons of
millionaires — are mere infants wandering around
in dreamland The State's Attorney should not discuss the gruesome details of the horrible crime in
their presence A kindly old nurse ought to tell
them a bedtime story They did not commit a murder, they broke a jar of jam in the pantry That
is not blood on their hands, it is jam

It has been suggested also that with the plea of
guilty entered the State should say no more, their
arguments must go without a reply Put away the
judicial slipper, do not spank these naughty boys,
let them go back to play They are not the intellectuals who say there is no God Oh, no, they still
believe in Santa Claus

Who but the State's Attorney could be so vicious
and cruel as to talk about the death penalty in a
case of this sort? Savage and Marshall should have
come up here and tried them with " kindness " and
" consideration "

I can imagine, your Honor, when this case was
called for trial and your Honor began to warn these
two defendants of the consequences of their plea,
and when you said we may impose the death penalty, Savage and Marshall both rushing up and
saying " Now, Judge! now, Judge! not so fast!
We don't intend to be cruel in this case We don't

intend to be harsh. We want to try these boys, these kiddies, with kindness and consideration. Your Honor ought not to shock their ears by such a cruel reference to the laws of this State, to the penalty of death. Why, don't you know that one of them has to shave every day of the week, and that is a bad sign? The other one has to shave twice a week only, and that is a bad sign. One is short and one is tall, and it is equally a bad sign in both of them. When they were children they played with Teddy bears. One of them has three moles on his back. One is over-developed sexually and the other not quite so good." If one of them had a hairlip I suppose Darrow would want me to apologize for having had them indicted.

Imagine Savage and Marshall making a plea of that sort to your Honor, and saying "Instead of sending these two mad boys, who are wandering around in the dark, to prison for life, parole them to us. Marshall will take 'Dickie' and Savage will take 'Babe.' And we will try to get them out of this 'fantasy life.'"

I know what your Honor would have said if they had pursued that line of conduct. You would have said 'Mr. Sheriff, search these men, find out how much money they have in their pockets.'"

And if no money were found in their pockets, your Honor would tell the sheriff to take them to the psychopathic hospital, and you would send for me and say "Crowe send up somebody who has some brains to prosecute a murder case in my court room'

If we are cold-blooded, we have, according to Mr Darrow, planned for three months, and conspired to take the lives of two little boys who are wandering around in dreamland We have been held up to the world as men who desire blood who have no kindly instincts within our hearts at all.

That is not fair to Tom Marshall, not fair to Joe Savage, both of whom have the respect and confidence of the people of this community

I have never been vicious nor cruel I believe in God — which may be considered a fault in this case not only by the two defendants but by the master pleader who represents them — and I believe in the laws of this State I believe the State's Attorney is as kindly a man as the paid "humanitarian' who believes in doing his fellow citizens good — after he has done them good and plenty.

I have a right to forgive those who trespass against me, as I do, in the hopes that I in the hereafter will be forgiven my trespasses As a private citizen I have that right, and as a private citizen I live that religion But, as a public official, I have no right to forgive those who violate their country's laws It is my duty to prosecute them

Your Honor has a right to, and I know you do forgive those who trespass against John R Caverly. But, sitting here as the Chief Justice of this great court, you have no right to forgive anybody who violates the law You have to deal with him as the law prescribes

And I want to say to your Honor, in this case, with the mass of evidence presented by the State if a jury were sitting in that box and returned a verdict and did not fix the punishment at death, every person in this community would feel that that verdict was founded in corruption And I will tell you why

Your Honor, I have taken quite a trip during the last four or five weeks I thought I was going to be kept in Chicago all summer trying this case, and that most of my time would be spent in the Criminal Court Building And I find I have been mistaken I did come up to your Honor's court room five weeks ago, and after I was there a little while Old Doc Yak — is that his name? — the man from Washington — oh, Dr White — took me by the hand and led me into the nursery of two poor, rich young boys, and he introduced me to a Teddy bear Then he told me some bedtime stories, and after I got through listening to them, he took me into the kindergarten and he presented to me little " Dickie " and " Babe," and he wanted to know if I had any objection to calling them that, and I said no, if he had no purpose

And after we had wandered between the nursery and the kindergarten for quite a while, I was taken in hand by the Bachrach brothers and taken to a psychopathic laboratory, and there I received quite

The Loeb-Leopold Case

a liberal education in mental diseases, and particularly what certain doctors did not know about them Three wise men from the East came to tell your Honor about these little babes, and, being three wise men brought on from the East, they want to make the picture a little more perfect. One of them was sacrilegious enough to say that Leopold, this pervert, this murderer, this kidnaper, thought that he was the Christ child and his mother the Madonna — and without a syllable of evidence to support the blasphemous statement

Who said that this young pervert ever thought he was the Christ child? He has proclaimed since he was eleven years of age that there is no God "The fool in his heart hath said there is no God" I wonder now, Nathan, whether you think there is a God or not I wonder whether you think it was pure accident that this disciple of Nietzschian philosophy dropped his glasses or whether it was an act of Divine Providence to visit upon your miserable carcasses the wrath of God in the enforcement of the laws of the State of Illinois.

After the Bachrachs had completed my education in the psychopathic laboratories, then my good friend Clarence Darrow took me on a Chautauqua trip, visiting various towns We would go to social settlements, such as the Hull House, and Clarence would expound his peculiar philosophy of life, and we would meet with communists and anarchists, and Clarence would regale them with his philosophy of the law, which means there ought not to be any law and there ought not to be any enforcement of the law And he even took me to Springfield, where he argued before the legislature that you ought to abolish capital punishment in the State of Illinois I don't know whether the fact that he had a couple of rich clients who were dangerously close to the gallows prompted that trip or not I know when he was a member of the legislature he did not abolish capital punishment nor introduce a bill for that purpose

Yes, and on this tour he criticised the State's Attorney of this county severely because he, in a humane way, wanted to correct the law so that men of this sort could be dealt with before somebody lay cold in death, and that the children of this community might be protected

When I occupied the position that your Honor now graces I had an unfortunate man come before me He was a man of my own race, of my own faith I don't know whether his pineal gland was calcified or ossified I don t know whether he had clubfeet or not, and I did not inspect his back to find out whether he had a couple of moles I don't know whether he developed sexually at 14 or 16 I knew under the law he had committed a dastardly crime He had taken a little six-year-old girl, a daughter of the poor, and he was a poor man, and he outraged her and he took her into the basement and covered her over with coal He did not even

The Loeb-Leopold Case

have the decency or the heart to put a handkerchief over that little dead face as he heaped the coal upon it

The law says in extreme cases death shall be the penalty If I were in the legislature I might vote against such a law I don't know But as a judge I have no right to set aside that law I have no right to defeat the will of the people, as expressed by the legislature of Illinois I have no right to be a judicial anarchist, even if Clarence Darrow is an anarchistic advocate He says that hanging does not stop murder I think he is mistaken From the time Thomas Fitzgerald expiated his crime upon the gallows, I have not heard of any little tot in Chicago who met a like fate to that which Janet Wilkinson met

I will direct your Honor's attention to the year 1920, when Judge Kavanagh, Judge Brentano, Judge Barrett and Judge Scanlan came over here at my request and from the fifth day of May until the first day of July tried nothing but murder cases In addition to the many men that they sent to the penitentiary for manslaughter, or a term of years for murder, in that brief period of less than sixty days, fifteen men were sentenced to death in the Criminal Court of Cook County The records of the Police Department, the records of the Chicago Crime Commission show that as the result of that murder fell 51 per cent in Cook County during the year 1920

We had a time here when every night in every newspaper there was a column devoted to the number of automobiles stolen. We established an automobile court, and I presided in it and after we had sent several hundred to penal institutions for stealing automobiles, the Rolls-Royce became as safe as the flivver on the streets of Chicago.

We had a reign of terror inaugurated here for years by criminals who dominated labor unions. They were above and beyond the law. They laughed at it, and spat in its face, just the same as these two poor young sons of multimillionaires. Forty-nine of them were convicted in the courts of Cook County. The building industry that had been strangled for years began to revive and take on life, and we have not heard anything of the Maders or the Murphys or the Walshes since.

You have heard a lot about England. Well, I was never very enthusiastic about England myself. That is due to heredity in me. I never had any liking or respect for her laws as they applied to my ancestors and people in an adjoining isle, but I have learned to have a wholesome respect for the manner in which they enforce the laws of England in England. Murder is murder there, it is not a fantasy. There, justice is handed out swiftly and surely, and as a result there are less murders in the entire Kingdom of Great Britain yearly than there are in this city alone.

May it please your Honor, we have heard considerable about split personalities in this case. I was somewhat surprised to find that my old friend, who has acted as counsel and as nurse in this case for the two babes who were wandering in dreamland, also was possessed of a split personality. I had heard so much of the milk of human kindness that ran out in streams from his large heart, that I was surprised to know he had so much poison in his system also.

It is wrong if your Honor please, for the State's Attorney and his two assistants to refer to these two perverts, these two atheists, these two murderers, in language that they can understand. But it is all right for Mr. Darrow to take an honorable physician, and to characterize him, without a shred of evidence, without the slightest foundation, as a peddler of perjury, and hurl that cruel charge broadcast over this land. Where is there anything in this case that warrants Clarence Darrow to make such an infamous charge against Dr. Krohn? I would suggest that if they want mercy, if they want charity, they practice a little bit of it.

Treat them with kindness and consideration? Call them babes? Call them children? Why, from the evidence in this case, if your Honor please, they are as much entitled to the sympathy and the mercy of this court as a couple of rattlesnakes flushed with venom, coiled, ready to strike. They are no good to themselves. The only purpose for which they are of any use is to debase themselves. They are a dis-

The Loeb-Leopold Case

grace to their honored families and they are a menace to this community. The only useful thing that remains for them now is to go out of this life and to go out of it as quickly as possible, under the law.

As I said we have been traveling considerably since this trial began. We have been through dreamland, we have been through the nursery. When I came into this court I thought the playthings of these two perverts were bloody chisels ropes gags, guns and acids. But one of those wise men from the East told me that I was mistaken, that their play toys are Teddy bears, soldiers' uniforms, police uniforms, and the toys that all healthy-minded children delight to play with.

We have been in psychopathic laboratories, we have been in hospitals, we have been before the legislature, and we have been addressing meetings of communists and expounding doctrines that I consider as dangerous as the crime itself. I think it is about time that we get back to the Criminal Court. I think it is about time that we realize that we are before the Chief Justice of this court, that we are engaged not in experiments, not in philosophical discussions, but we are back here trying the murder case of the age, the details of which fill with horror.

But Mr Darrow says "These poor little sons of multimillionaires It is their wealth that is their misfortune, if it were not for their wealth, there would be no interest in this case"

The Loeb-Leopold Case

Yet, fifty years ago the Ross boy was kidnaped — not the son of a multimillionaire. He was never found. And yet we all, even those of us born many years after, still talk about the case of Charley Ross. There is something in the nature of the crime itself that arrests the attention of every person in the land. A child is stolen, the heart of every mother, the heart of every father, the heart of every man who has a heart goes out to the parents of that child.

Bobby Franks kidnaped! When we had not the slightest information who was guilty of the dastardly crime, the papers were full of it. It was the only topic of conversation. It remained the only topic of conversation for a week before the State's Attorney of this county called in Nathan Leopold, Jr.

Their wealth, in my judgment, has nothing to do with this. It permits a defense here seldom given to men in the Criminal Court. Take away the millions of the Loebs and Leopolds, and Clarence Darrow's tongue is as still as the tongue of Julius Caesar. Take away their millions, and the wise men from the East would not be here to tell you about fantasies, Teddy bears, and about bold boys who had their pictures taken in cowboy uniform. Take away their money, and what happens? The same as has happened to all other men who have been tried in this building that had no money: a plea of guilty, a police officer sworn, a coroner's physician sworn, the parents of the murdered boy sworn, a sentence

The Loeb-Leopold Case

I used to wonder what the poet Gray meant when he talked about the short and simple annals of the poor. Clarence Darrow once said that the poor man on trial was usually disposed of in fifteen minutes, but if he was rich and committed some crime, and he got a good lawyer, his trial would last twenty-one days. Well, they have three good lawyers, and it has lasted just a little bit longer, and in addition they had three wise men from the East.

Are we trying here, if your Honor please, a murder case? And what is the evidence presented by the State upon which we ask the extreme penalty? A murder. Was it the result of a drunken brawl, a murder committed in hot blood? Some injury, real or fanciful? A man shooting down another because he debauched his wife and destroyed his home? A murder the result of impulse or passion?

No, one of the most carefully planned murders that your Honor or I, from all our long experience, have ever heard about. Was it a murder committed by some young gamin of the streets, whose father was a drunkard and his mother loose, who was denied every opportunity and brought up in the slums, never a decent example set before him? No, but a murder committed by two superintellects, coming from the members of the most respected families in Chicago, every advantage that love, wealth and position could give them was theirs.

A man's conduct, I believe, your Honor, depends upon his philosophy of life. Those who want to grow up to be useful and respected citizens in the community have a correct philosophy of life Those who want to excel in crime, those who want to tear down instead of build up, select the wrong philosophy of life That is all there is to this They had the power of choice, and they deliberately chose to adopt the wrong philosophy and to make their conduct correspond with it

These two defendants were perverts, Loeb the victim and Leopold the aggressor, and they quarreled Then they entered into a "childish compact," Dr Healy says, so that these unnatural crimes might continue Dr Healy says that this is a "childish compact', and I say if Dr Healy is not ashamed of himself, he ought to be My God! I was a grown man before I knew of such depravity Mr Bachrach says that is an evidence of insanity The statute of Illinois says that crimes against nature are crimes punishable by imprisonment in the penitentiary It is not a defense to a murder charge

Mitigation! Mitigation! I have heard so many big words in this case that I sometimes thought probably we were letting error creep into the record So many strange, foreign words have been used here, and the Constitution provides that the trial must be conducted in the English language I don't know, maybe I have got aggravation and mitigation mixed up

It is a mitigating circumstance, if your Honor please, that when they were outlining the plan of this conspiracy and murder, they wanted to take a little girl, the daughter of the rich, and first rape her and then murder her, and then collect the ransom. If that evidence had been put in by the State, I would have thought it was an aggravation. These three wise men, with their distorted theories, hired by the defense, put that evidence in. Clarence Darrow calls it a mitigating circumstance. Why, when they murder a boy they ought to be treated with kindness and consideration. If they had taken a little girl, and debauched her, I suppose each would have been entitled to a medal.

What have we come to in this community? I want to tell your Honor bearing in mind the testimony that was whispered into your ear one of the motives in this case was a desire to satisfy unnatural lust. They first wanted a little girl so Leopold could rape her, then they decided on a little boy. What happened? Immediately upon killing him they took his trousers off. And how do you undress a child? First, the little coat, the collar, the tie, the shirt, and the last thing the trousers. And yet immediately after killing this poor little boy, his trousers alone came off and for three hours that little dead boy, with all his other clothes on him, remained in that car, and they did not take the balance of the clothes off until they pulled the body into the culvert.

Away back in November, if your Honor please, when this crime first began to take the form of a

The Loeb-Leopold Case

kidnaping for ransom, it was necessary to write some letters. These two little boys, wandering around in dreamland, knew what very few boys and very few men know that it is possible to take a typewritten document and tell what kind of a machine it is written on. So they go to Ann Arbor and they steal a typewriter, a portable typewriter, for the purpose of writing these letters on it, and they go along working out the details of this crime.

Mr Darrow says that there is no motive, that this is a senseless crime, that the $10,000 had nothing to do with it. I will undertake to prove, not by argument, but by sworn testimony that the $10,000 had much to do with it. I will show that this was not the crime of diseased emotion, but a crime planned in all its minuteness by more than ordinary intellect.

Dr Healy, on his cross-examination, testified as follows

Q Do you regard this as a crime of passion? *A* No, sir

Q It is a cold-blooded proposition, premeditated and planned? *A* Yes, sir.

Q Now, Doctor, if in the inception of this crime it is admitted in evidence that the first thing the defendants did was to steal a typewriter so it would be difficult for the authorities to trace the letters written, would you consider that a form of childish fantasy, or would you consider that a result of their intellectual attainments? *A* It is the result of their intellectual attainments, in my opinion

The Loeb-Leopold Case

Q And if, after having procured the typewriter, they bought a block of paper, plain paper, so that it would be difficult or impossible to trace it, and wrote the letters on that, would that be the fantasy working, or their normal intellect? *A* I think it was very good intellect working

Q If, after having written a letter, the defendants destroyed the remaining sheets of paper by burning them, and attempted to destroy or lose the typewriter, by throwing it into the water, after removing the keys and throwing them in a different part of the lake, was that boyish fantasy in operation or was it their good intellects? *A* I think it was all part and parcel of their desire and plan to commit a perfect crime

Q Now, intellect is sometimes commonly referred to as good horse sense, isn't it? *A* I think it is their intellect working I don't know about the horse sense, but it is their intellect

Q Well, good common sense? *A* I don't think they are showing much common sense in committing the crime at all, you see, but, having started on it, they used very good intellect

Q Was it intellect or fantasy that caused them to assume the name of Morton D Ballard, and rent a room in the Morrison Hotel under that name? *A* Undoubtedly their intellect working

Q After having given the name of Morton D Ballard, the address at the Morrison Hotel, the name of Louis Mason as a Chicago reference, was it childish fantasy that caused Loeb to remain at the telephone booth on Wabash Avenue, the number of which Leopold had given to the Rent-a-Car people, to wait for him to call on Louis Mason, was that fantasy or intellect working? *A* Undoubtedly intellect

Q Was it intellect working when they opened a

The Loeb-Leopold Case

bank account at the Hyde Park State Bank under the name of Morton D Ballard and gave that as the bank reference? *A* I think it was

Q Was it intellect, or boyish, childish fantasy working, when they took the bloody rope that they had wrapped the body in and saturated it with gasoline and took it to the lake to burn? *A* I think it was their intellect

Q Was it intellect or fantasy working when they attempted to rub the bloodstains from the rented car? *A* Intellect, I believe

Q In other words, every detail of this crime is a crime of intellect, and not a fantasy? *A* I think so

Q And they are above the average intellect? *A* One of them is, the other is not

Q The other is not? *A* I think he is just about average

Q And so superintellect in one case and normal intellect in one case planned and carried out every detail of this crime? *A* I think so

Q Was it intellect or childish fantasy that caused Leopold to try to divert suspicion prior to his arrest to other persons? *A* It was his intellect that worked

Q Was it intellect or fantasy that caused Leopold to lie for two days to the State's Attorney of this county when first brought in? *A* Intellect

Q Was it intellect or fantasy that caused Loeb when brought to the State's Attorney to lie for a considerable period of time? *A* I think it was his intellect

Q Now were there any other emotions acting in conjunction with the intellect when they attempted to cover up this crime by the various things they did and by the various lies they told? *A* It would be hard for me to say whether there was or not or whether it was, very largely, an intellectual process

There is two hundred and fifty dollars' worth of testimony. I wondered when I heard these doctors say that they could not make a complete adequate examination in less than twenty or thirty days, whether the fact that they were working on a per diem rate of two hundred and fifty dollars did not enter into the matter.

The State was peculiarly fortunate in this case, in that we took time by the forelock. Mr. Bachrach, Jr., was guileless enough to believe that after I had gotten their confessions and corroborated them in every detail, I had a suspicion in my mind that these two young perverts and murderers were insane. Mr. Darrow knows me a little longer, and he is not quite so guileless as the younger Bachrach, and he guessed that maybe after I knew they had no defense on the fact, and knew how much money they had, I might think that they were going to put in some kind of a fancy insanity defense. And that is the reason I sent for the four best alienists in Chicago, while I still had these young, egotistical Smart Alecs — that is all they are, they are not supermen, they are just a couple of spoiled Smart Alecs, spoiled by the twaddling and petting of their folks and by the people who fawn upon them on account of their wealth. They repeat, parrotlike, things that they have remembered and assume the solemn expression of an owl and talk about supermen. In one breath one of these wise men from the East will tell you that the two defendants still believe in Santa Claus, and then in the next breath Mr. Darrow will tell you that they do not believe even in God

What better opportunity in God's world has the State ever had in an examination than was had in this, from 2 30 until 6 30, and these two young Smart Alecs were telling their story and boasting of their depravity before they had been advised to invent insanity, before they had been advised to answer certain questions in certain ways, and before they had been advised to withhold, even from the wise men of the East, certain information that might be detrimental to the defense in this case? Yes, as Doctor Krohn said their souls were bare Every incident that they told me about I put a witness on the stand to prove Every detail of their confession has been corroborated by sworn testimony and by exhibits offered in evidence

And, if your Honor please, I don't think that there are a lot of things that we have to have alienists for I don't think that it is necessary, in a majority of cases for you or for me, or for other men experienced in the practice of the criminal law, to call in an alienist to find out whether John Jones, the author of this handwriting, also wrote that In a great many cases we can tell by looking at them whether they were written by the same person I am not the physician that the younger Bachrach is, I am not the philosopher that the senior counsel is, but I think that if I talk to a man for four hours

The Loeb-Leopold Case

consecutively and he is insane, I am going to have a pretty good suspicion of it, and I believe if your Honor watches a man for thirty days, day in and day out, and he is a lunatic, you are going to have a well defined suspicion of it

When the learned doctor who had been employed to find out just how crazy these two fellows were got on the stand, he was probably instructed "Just make them crazy enough so they won't hang, but don't make them crazy enough to make it necessary to put this up to twelve men because twelve men are not going to be fooled by your twaddle Just make them insane enough so it will make a mitigating circumstance that we can submit to the court"

One of these wise men was asked

Q Doctor, do you know that Leopold has written a great deal upon the subject of ornithology, that he is one of the authorities on that subject in the United States, that he has lectured before the students of Harvard University upon that subject? A Yes sir; I do

Q Did you see his work? A Yes

Q Did you read that? A No

Q You were employed to examine that man, weren't you? A Yes

Q What did you do? A I examined his urine

Q Don t you think you could get a better idea of his mental condition by reading the things that he wrote, the product of his brain, than you could by examining his urine A I don t know

Now, probably he just wanted to find out how much sugar he could discover to lay a foundation for an argument by Clarence Darrow that these two boys were too sweet for your Honor to treat as you would the ordinary criminal

I was discussing the testimony of the four State alienists, concededly four of the best alienists in the city of Chicago, and the reason that the State's Attorney, in his effort to enforce the law effectively, called them in on Sunday, before the defendants were taken out of his custody and turned over to their lawyers and the sheriff, was to prevent a perjured defense by their friends, associates and servants, I called in every person that I understood knew either one of these boys, at once, and placed them under oath and asked them what they knew about the mental condition of the defendants

If I had not the defense in this case would have been insanity and not a mental disease that goes all around insanity in order to avoid a jury trial

I don't wonder that the senior counsel, in his wisdom gained through many years of practice, made the proposition to the State, when he found out what the State had done in the way of preparation " Don't you call any of your lay witnesses, and I won't call any of mine " I told him " Bring on your lay witnesses The law is well fortified " And after he got through with Miss Nathan, he was through with all the rest

Don't overlook these facts the State's alienists say, in addition to the matters and things that they

The Loeb-Leopold Case

learned, that they took into consideration every bit of Dr Hulbert's report, just the same as the three wise men from the East did Not only that, they took into consideration all the testimony of these three wise men They didn't overlook a word, they didn't overlook the fact that one shaved every day and the other one shaved twice a week, they even considered the little Teddy and the cowboy suit And from it all they found no evidence of mental disease

The only explanation I can give of the testimony of Dr White is that he is in his second childhood I would hate to think a man of his attainments would prostitute his profession and prostitute his learning to tell the story that he told here

One of the very significant things the eminent doctor says was that little Dick had his picture taken in a cowboy's uniform when he was four years of age, and that is a distinguishing thing and stamped him as one of diseased mind with homicidal tendencies and I saw a shudder go through every woman in the court room that has a " kid " four or five years of age, and I began to think of my four " kids " I suppose Marshall Field's sale of cowboy suits must have fallen off at least one hundred thousand since that doctor testified

When the other doctors saw how ridiculous and silly it all was, they said they paid no attention to it, and one by one, each doctor discarded this silly bosh that the preceding doctor had testified to as distinguishing matter, and finally the Grand Old — the gland old — Man of the Defense, Clarence Darrow, seeing how absolutely absurd it was, substituted as a defense in this case his peculiar philosophy of life, of which we will talk later on

They put on Dr Hulbert to testify about certain glands, ductless and otherwise, and your Honor heard an eminent authority upon that subject, Dr Woodyatt, and he said there is so little known about the pineal gland and about these other matters and things that this other doctor testified to so glibly, that nobody knew what effect it would have upon the mind of a person, that a calcified gland existed in a sane, sound mind, the same as it did in a diseased mind, and that all the testimony of Dr Hulbert upon that proposition was as illuminating and valuable as that of Old Doc Yak with his Teddy bears and Buffalo Bill suits

If these men are insane, I ask your Honor why they were instructed not to let our alienists examine them further

Mr Darrow I object to that statement, there is no such evidence, and no evidence that you ever asked for it

Mr Crowe It is in evidence, if your Honor please, that when they were in my office Monday and Dr Singer was there, they replied to all questions "On advice of counsel we decline to answer" If the defense was a heavy cancer, why should not they bare their breasts and let every doctor and layman look on and see it? If there is a diseased mind why tell Dr Singer ' On advice of counsel, we respectfully decline to answer ' ? Are they honest in their defense? Or are they trying to put something over on the court?

Mr Darrow Pardon me There is nowhere any evidence that Dr. Singer ever asked any questions, or that they were ever asked for any examination by Dr Singer or by any other alienist which they did not allow

[A recess was here taken until the following morning when Mr Crowe resumed his argument]

Mr Crowe May it please your Honor, last night I was talking about the State alienists and the three wise men from the East who came here to testify that the little ' Babe, ' or the little babes, rather, were suffering from a diseased mind But no one has been able to give this mental disease a name And yet everyone who got on the stand for the defense pretended to know all that there was in the books and a great deal that never got into the books

I was surprised that Old Doc White wasn t able to name the peculiar mental disease he says exists here, because he in the past has been able to invent names for diseases which did not exist If your Honor will recollect, I questioned him as to whether or not he was the same William A White who testified in the case of *Gonzales vs the United States,* and he said he was. There he was trying to save a man from death.

Mr Bachrach: I object, if your Honor please, to any argument based upon the Gonzales case, upon the ground that your Honor specifically refused to let us show our side of the case, and your Honor stated at that time you did not care what occurred in the Gonzales case.

Mr Crowe: If we can quote poetry and if we can quote philosophy, I do not know why I cannot quote law.

Mr Darrow: That is not quoting law.

Mr Crowe: I called their attention to the case, and identified the doctor as having testified in it, and in their argument they could have argued anything they wanted to about it. They have argued every other case that was tried in the Criminal Court of Cook County. There was a man in prison, and Dr White was trying to save him from the gallows, and he said he had a " prison psychosis." That is, he was afraid, he was scared stiff that he was going to hang. And the United States Court says that the opinion is expressed that the prisoner is suffering from " prison psychosis," a newly discovered type of mental disease or insanity. Discovered by Dr White.

The court quotes Dr White as saying that the theory of malingering does not entirely explain the situation. " He also says that a previous attack of mental disturbance let up very shortly after he had been sent to Daunemora. This evidently refers to a former conviction in some other jurisdiction, after which he had been committed to an insane asylum. And he adds (quoting Doctor White) 'In all probability this present disturbance would all disappear very rapidly if the causes for its existence were removed.'"

In all probability the present mental disease of these two defendants would disappear very rapidly if the causes for its existence were removed. If the glasses had never been found, if the State's Attorney had not fastened the crime upon these two defendants, Nathan Leopold would be over in Paris or some other of the gay capitals of Europe, indulging his unnatural lust with the $5,000 he had wrung from Jacob Franks. If they were to be discharged today, through some technicality in the law, this present disturbance would all disappear very rapidly, if the causes for its existence were removed. I used to wonder why they got Doc White — and this explains it.

Now, if your Honor please, we will go back of this defense, and see whether it is an honest defense or not, see whether these mental disturbances came on as suddenly as they would disappear if the causes of them were removed. Your Honor will recollect that while doctors employed by the defense were sitting in the court room, witnesses were put on to testify to fainting spells. The purpose of that was to lay a foundation, in my judgment, for some doctor to later take the stand and testify that Loeb was suffering from epilepsy, and it would be argued that, having epilepsy, his mind was diseased

Dr Hulbert, in his report, as I will later show you, says that there were not any evidences of fainting in Loeb, except one fainting spell that he had during initiation and yet witness after witness was put on, and they testified that he fainted, that his eyes were glassy and that he frothed at the mouth But cross-examination showed that he was merely drunk, he was not rigid, but he was stiff, his frothing at the mouth was a drunken vomit

The evidence further showed that these other fainting spells were due to the fact that, in one case, seven or eight large boys jumped on him, and he fainted as the result of injuries inflicted upon him, he fainted again in the hospital after he had been in an automobile accident, and the doctor who waited upon him said that the fainting spells were due entirely in his judgment to the accident Then the doctor who had been employed to take the stand and testify to epilepsy was dismissed If these lay witnesses had stood up, and had not broken down under cross-examination, that doctor would have testified to epilepsy

I submit that this defense is not an honest defense This is a defense built up to meet the needs of the case If the State had only had half of the evidence that it did have, or a quarter of the evidence that it had, we would have had a jury in the

The Loeb-Leopold Case

box, and a plea of not guilty. But trapped like a couple of rats, with no place to escape except through an insanity defense, they proceed to build it up.

A weird, uncanny crime? The crime is not as weird or uncanny as the defense that is put in here. Let us see what Dr. Hulbert said in his report. That is in evidence, introduced by the defense, so I do not suppose there will be any objection to my reading from that. I am glad that the defendants' lawyers concede me some few rights in this court room, although they argue that I ought to be down in the office, after a plea of guilty, and that I have no business up here at all.

The report: "Personal history, Richard Loeb. Mother's health. During pregnancy she was not very sick. Her fever was not remarkable, although there was much morning sickness."

The doctor did not testify to that on direct examination, your Honor. He did not think this report would ever get into the hands of the State's Attorney, and he said he did not. He created the impression by his direct examination that there was something wrong at the time of this boy's birth.

What does he say in his report? He was a perfect baby. Oh! He developed a little late sexually, and at the age of fifteen Dr. Hulbert in his report said he had gonorrhea.

On page nine: "There is no history of fainting

attacks except that once during an initiation ceremony at school he fainted "

In other words, after considering the Teddy bears and the Buffalo Bill suits, and all this other trash that was testified to by these wise men from the East, counsel or somebody decided that they had to add something more to it to make it stand even as a mitigating circumstance, and while their report said that there was no history of fainting attacks except once, they tried to prove a dozen in order to build a foundation for epilepsy

Then this nurse, the nurse who, according to the testimony of the defense, knew more about Richard Loeb up until the time he was fourteen years of age than any living person They tried to create the impression that she was insane, and that Dick caught his insanity from her, the same as one boy catches measles from another They had her here in Chicago and she is not produced as a witness A letter was read to indicate that she was insane, and if I ever read a letter that more clearly demonstrated sanity than the letter written by that nurse, I don't remember it It was a kindly, loving letter, sent by a woman to a boy she loved, filled with motherly advice, advice that it develops is so sadly needed in this case by these two young perverts

A picture was introduced of her to show that she was some terribly hideous creature Let us see what Dr Hulbert says about her " She returned to Chicago after the arrest of young Richard to help him in any way she could, and through the attorneys arrangements were made for an interview She is very reserved, quiet and strict, her memory is good She is a woman of attractive appearance, modestly and carefully dressed She denied any imperfections in herself while with the boy during her stay with the family She said that he was quite all right at 15 years of age at the time she left the house She said he was a lazy boy, but a bright student He was lazy until he got along in several grades at school where he found that he could graduate in one year's less time than he expected, if he would study, and so he began to study hard She denied that he ever had fears or any disorder in his sleep She would not say anything which might reflect on the boy even though she was plainly told that a complete understanding of this boy was essential for an accurate diagnosis"

She came on here, as Dr Hulbert said, to do anything within her power to help the boy, short of perjury, although she was told that a complete understanding of the boy was essential for a correct diagnosis which means for a defense in this case, she would not say anything that might reflect upon him because she intended to tell the truth and that is why she was sworn as a witness before these alienists, but was not brought into court and sworn before your Honor

It has been argued here that because Richard Loeb told the doctors that he had no ambition in life, that he hadn't selected or thought of any profession, that is an indication he is mentally unbalanced, and because the other defendant had a definite ambition in life, he is also mentally unbalanced

A happy philosophy of medicine, especially when you are testifying in a guilty case, and trying to cheat the gallows It is too bad that they have two defendants here It would be so much easier to prove one insane, because anything you found in him could be a bad sign. But when you have two, and they are not exactly alike, when one has broken arches and the other has a high arch, why, then, it has got to be a bad sign in one and a bad sign in the other And if one has to shave every day, that is a bad sign, and if the other does not have to shave but twice a week, that is a bad sign It was a bad sign that Richard Loeb did not have any definite aim or purpose in life, and it was also a bad sign because Leopold wanted to study law and ornithology

Well, let us see what Dr Hulbert says about this "When the patient" — that is Loeb — ' was asked about what use he expected to make of his education, and what were his ambitions, he stated he expected to study law the next year He said he had always intended to study law "

And yet when they were putting on their defense, everybody had him wandering around like a ship without a rudder, and not knowing what port he was going to put into

"At one time he had thought of teaching history, but he felt that he was not of the scholarly type Asked why, he replied that he was always lazy, and that he could never sit down and apply himself As a boy, he poisoned his mind by reading detective stories"

Well, therein is where a whole lot of us are in the same fix I remember crawling under the bed to read Nick Carter After I got through reading Nick Carter I began to read Gaboriau's French detective stories, and when I was a student of Yale I paid more attention to Raffles than I did to real property

Oh, the only reason that Dickie committed this slight delinquency of murdering little Bobby Franks was that he desired the thrill, all his life he craved for thrills

What do Bowman and Hulbert say about it? "He never appeared to crave a thrill or excitement, but was rather quiet in his conduct, after Miss Struthers left that home he seemed to be much the same as before, quiet rather affectionate, extremely polite and respectful"

That is what the friends and members of the family must have told the doctor Here is what the patient told the doctor himself "The patient's estimate of himself While also at times he had a tremendous output of energy and physical ability, he tired easily He is rather inclined to be a leader in athletics and games which he enjoys "

Why, the whole trouble with him is that he never led the natural life that boys lead He was always kept in the house with his nose buried in some serious, solemn volume That is what we were told And the only time he had any boys was when Doc White could put some interpretation upon those boys which would lead to the conclusion of a diseased mind That is why we heard about the Teddy bears and these various suits of his He never went out and played as boys play baseball, marbles and other things, and yet when he is talking to the doctor and the doctor reports to the three wise men from the East, he says he is inclined to be a leader in athletics and games, which he enjoys.

"He makes friends very easily and feels quite at ease with strangers He is inclined to be a leader and likes to dominate his environments."

Well, isn't that natural? Everybody desires to strive, to succeed and to lead But the doctor adds, " but can fit himself easily into any sort of a situation so that he does not become bothered or upset if some one else happens to be dominating the very situation and he is compelled to assume a minor rôle "

Also. "While the patient often acts without reflection and is quite impulsive, he nevertheless plans a great deal and works out consistent schemes for the future."

He plans a great deal and works out consistent schemes for the future — this mad brain of this mad boy!

"He is open and frank with others as long as he feels there is nothing he wants to conceal"

Dr White said he couldn't lie to him 'Nobody can lie to me I can read their minds just the same as a doctor can look into the human body with an X-ray'

Well, I don't suppose he thinks he knows more than the Lord does, but I don't believe he would concede that the Lord knew any more than he does when the Lord was his age

"But if he feels that it is to his interest to hold back something he does so He therefore gives an appearance of great frankness, which is not true The patient says that he will tell a lie with no compunction whatever, and that he is completely dishonest"

Let us see whether he lied to these doctors and withheld information, the same as they lied to your Honor and withheld information Here again the doctor says, talking about his being tied to the apron strings of an old nurse and never being allowed to play as other boys played page 41 "He has always been fond of athletics and outdoors sports such as tennis, swimming hockey skating and so forth He is considered an extremely good bridge player and has spent a great deal of time playing it He is fond of dancing and mixed society He has used alcohol considerably since he was 15 and gotten drunk a number of times "

Never permitted to play with other boys, never allowed the recreation that other boys had, and yet Dr Hulbert said on page 42 " In 1912 at the age of seven, he and Jack Mandel built a five-foot-square room with a pointed roof This was used as a playhouse A year or so later the boys formed a guinea pig company and used the playhouse for the office of the company In 1916 Richard Loeb, with five or six other boys, published two issues of a small three-by-five-inch 24-page journal, called *Richard's Magazine* His contribution was that of being editor, manager and author His writings showed quite advanced thinking for a boy of his age, and reflected well the humanitarian environment of his home "

Reflected the humanitarian environment of his home, and yet Mr Darrow in a vain effort to save their worthless lives has said that they committed this murder on account of their families

Oh, another interesting thing that leads these wise men to think that they are demented and stark mad is that over in jail, while he is preparing his defense, he wants to wear an old ragged coat

" He has always been careful of his personal appearance and neat and clean about his person and has liked to appear well dressed He has always had a pleasant consciousness of his own body "

We are talking about the poor little rich boy who

had been brought up in a golden cage, and never had a chance to use his wings as other boys did And again I find in Dr Hulbert's report " He has always been interested in camping and motor boating and outdoor life in general This has never been linked with any intellectual pursuit such as botany, zoology or the like'

Tennis, swimming hockey, skating, bridge, dancing, all the sports every healthy, natural boy would like to indulge in, but a great many of which many are not able to indulge in, being the rich boys of poor parents and not the poor boys of multimillionaires

They didn't lie when questioned by their alienists It would not have done them any good to lie to Dr White anyhow But they did not lie to any of them, and they will testify that if they had lied, an impossible thing and if the things that they had told them had been false and that they had held back certain things that were material, they would have changed their opinion Oh, undoubtedly, if the facts were not as they are we would come to a different conclusion But these boys were collaborating with us while we were planning this weird, uncanny defense for them They didn t lie and they didn't withhold anything

Well, let's see what this report says " During the examination and his recitation of his criminal career he was not quite frank Without any indication facially or otherwise he would lie and repress certain instances, unless he imagined that the doctor was previously aware of those instances When questioned about this later he said he had failed to mention certain things because he thought it advisable not to mention them or because he had been advised not to mention them "

After some guileless attorney, studied in the medicine and grounded in it probably more than he is in the practice of criminal law, some doctor or some member of the family had gotten these two Smart Alecs and had trained and prepared them and told them what to tell the doctors and what not to tell them, then they bring out these doctors and say " Now, go in and listen to that story and if, after you listen to the story they tell you, you don't think they are crazy then you must be crazy "

" His older brother Allen does not know of these untold stories, but the patient says he will not tell them unless Allen advises him so to do "

What are these untold stories? They were not going to lie in order to fool the doctors, so that the doctors could fool your Honor No They were perfectly frank As Dr White said " They didn't lie to me and they wouldn't lie to a man as smart as I am " They had no thought when they were talking to the doctors as to their defense in this case, none whatever They might as a result of a childish phantasy murder little Bobby Franks as they wandered along in the dark, but God forbid that they should attempt to fool your Honor in an effort to save their lives

But let us continue from the Hulbert-Bowman report "On the other hand there is a certain legal advantage in minimizing the broadcasting of his episodes, even keeping them secret from his attorneys, examiners or relatives Consequently no great effort should be made to bring forth details which he wilfully suppresses"

This is Dr Bowman and Dr Hulbert advising Dr White, Dr Glueck and Dr Healy

Now, I quite agree with Dr Hulbert that when he wrote this report he never thought it was going to be read by the State's Attorney

"His phantasies usually occurred between the time of retiring and the time sleep comes over him He estimates that this period was on an average of a half an hour's duration"

Not wandering around all day, Mr Darrow, in a daydream and indulging in phantasies walking up and down the street snapping fingers, pointing out buildings, waving the gang here and there, not a phantasy that became a part of his life

Dr Hulbert and Dr. Bowman said that the phantasies usually occur a half hour before he goes to sleep That is the time your Honor and I and everybody else have phantasies When we get into bed we dream dreams of what we are going to accomplish and we scheme and plan, and that is exactly what Dickie Loeb did All this other stuff that we have been regaled with is perjury, pure and simple, perjury for a purpose. From Philip drunk to Philip sober, from the lying alienist on the stand to a report made by the alienist that they did not think would come to light.

Now, continuing on page 93 "He denied being implicated in the so-called gland robbery of Mr Ream." Well, it would be unfortunate with all of these old gland doctors and all this piffle about glands, that Dickie beat the doctors to it and experimented on glands prior to this time.

"He denied being in Geneva in the case of a ragged stranger who was found dead with his hands cut off and his face mutilated. He denied having participated in any other delinquencies." And mark you this, your Honor "But later referred to four episodes for which the letters A, B, C and D were suggested." He referred to four episodes. Four crimes, if your Honor please, merely designated as A, B, C and D. And the two doctors, whose only interest is to tell the truth as they find it, add in their own language "It was found forensically —'" now, what does forensically mean? That it was found from a legal standpoint, as the doctor said, "forensically inadvisable to question him about these."

What strange hold did this man Leopold have upon Loeb? Why did he submit himself to the unnatural practices of Leopold? I will tell you, your Honor, and I think I will demonstrate it beyond a

The Loeb-Leopold Case

peradventure of a doubt, that these four episodes, that these four crimes were known to Leopold, and he blackmailed Loeb, he threatened Loeb with exposure if he did not submit to him and Loeb had to go along with Leopold And Leopold was willing to go along with Loeb because he could use his body for vile and unnatural practices And I will prove that, and I will prove that by the testimony of the defense beyond a reasonable doubt

' On their way back from Ann Arbor " (on page 98) " the plan of kidnaping a boy coupled with the idea of ransom was first broached by the patient " That is the first time that Loeb talked to Leopold about kidnaping for ransom Not a thrill, but ransom And I will demonstrate that money was the motive here I will demonstrate that they gambled and they played for such high stakes that even their millionaire companions could not play with them I will demonstrate that they had money that they cannot account for unless it was the proceeds of A, B, C or D

" The patient had a definite boy in mind at that time The patient did not like this boy or his family " So says this report

A crime by mad boys without a purpose, without any thought of revenge, without any thought of money? Let's see The first boy they contemplated killing was a boy he did not like Hatred, revenge, was the motive in his mind at that time, but a desire for money overcame that

The Loeb-Leopold Case

"He was the patient's own age, rather large for his age The patient's idea was to get hold of this boy when he was coming back from a party and lure him into an automobile Neither of them, however, could think of any simple, certain way of securing the money They continued to discuss the matter, weighing the pros and cons, suggesting methods only to pick flaws in them In March, 1924, the patient conceived the idea of securing"— what? Thrill? Excitement? No "Conceived the idea of securing the money by having it thrown off of a moving train It was figured out first that the money should be thrown off of a moving train when it was dark somewhere in the country He and his companion spent many uncomfortable afternoons —" (I really sympathize with you dear little boys for all the discomfort you have suffered on those afternoons It is too bad that in this weird uncanny scheme of yours of murder, you had to spend many uncomfortable afternoons) — " going over the Illinois Central tracks looking for suitable location " Mad boys in the dark and dreamland, doing a mad act without any thought of the consequences of it, and not considering their personal safety at all? Too crazy to know that it was wrong and too crazy to care whether they were caught?

"They both felt that it was not safe to use either of their own cars The patient developed an intense interest in the plan and found also that it gave him a very pleasant topic of conversation when he and

The Loeb-Leopold Case

his companion were together drinking or driving about Patient's companion suggested that they rent a car, so they went to the Morrison Hotel and registered under the name of Ballard Letters were sent to Mr Ballard at the hotel and a bank account was opened in his name "

Here is a man who has no emotion, all intellect and no emotion His nurse says he was kind and affectionate, obedient and respectful Isn t that emotion? Isn't love one of the greatest emotions that surge through your heart? Kind and affectionate, loving What does the doctor say? " The bank account was opened in his name," and then the doctor adds in parenthesis " When the patient came to this point in the narrative he looked decidedly interested, drew up his chair, talked almost in a dramatic whisper with considerable tension, his eyes constantly roaming the room "

Whom are you going to believe? The doctor, after he has been coached, taking the stand and saying he has not any emotions, or the doctor in the first instance when he is making a report that he does not expect you or me to see?

And this document is offered in mitigation of the crime As I said yesterday, probably I have been confused by the use of all these learned terms in a foreign language that I did not understand or learn But if this is mitigation, I would like to know what is aggravation

" The patient's companion " — that is Leopold

—" first suggested that they get a girl Then they considered half a dozen boys, any one of them would do, that they were physically small enough to be easily handled "

" One who was physically small enough to be easily handled, whose parents were extremely wealthy, and would have no difficulty or disinclination to pay ransom money "

What is the motive? All the way through this report, all the way through the confessions, money, ransom, wealth

" Since they planned to kidnap a boy who was known to them, because it would be easy to lure him into their automobile, they felt that it was necessary to kill him at once to avoid any possible identification of themselves by the victim should he escape or their plans go awry."

That is the motive here The kidnaping was planned for ransom They wanted the money first, and they were going to kidnap a boy to get the money Then, to make sure they were picking the right fellow, whose folks were wealthy and who could pay the ransom, they had to pick a boy they knew and who knew them Then the motive for the murder was their own self-preservation You do not have to take my word for it, take the word of the doctors hired by the defense who say the boys told them that, themselves

Was this killing done, as we have been asked to believe, by the defense, merely for the thrill, your

Honor, or the excitement? What does the doctor further say on that? "The patient" (Loeb) "did not anticipate the actual killing with any pleasure"

It was not for the thrill or the excitement. The original crime was the kidnaping for money. The killing was an afterthought, to prevent their identification and their subsequent apprehension and punishment. He said he did not anticipate the killing with any pleasure. It was merely necessary in order to get the money. Motive? "The killing apparently has no other significance"—now, this is not my argument, your Honor, but on page 103 of their own report, their own evidence—"the killing apparently has no other significance than being an inevitable part of a perfect crime in covering one possible trace of identification."

That is the motive for the murder self-preservation, the same as a thief at night in your house, when suddenly surprised, shoots to kill.

See whether the mere wantonness of killing gave them the thrill that you are asked to believe. The report says "They anticipated a few unpleasant minutes in strangling him." Not the thrill and the delight and the fast-beating heart that they tell you Dickie Loeb has—if he has any heart at all. No.

And I might tell you at this point, your Honor, that the original plan of Loeb was not to kill him with a chisel, but they were to strangle him to death with the ropes that they procured. He was to pull one end and Leopold the other, and the reason he wanted that done was, as I will demonstrate as we go on, Leopold had something on him Leopold knew about the crimes A, B, C and D, and in this murder he was going to make Leopold pull the rope, so he would have something equal on Leopold

"And they planned for each of them, namely, the patient and his associate, to have hold of one end of the strangling rope, and they would pull at the same time so that both would be equally guilty of murder They did not seem to think that this would give them a closer tie in their friendship"

No thrill, no delight, it was the sharing of culpability

"It was not anticipated that the blow on the back of the head with the taped chisel would be fatal The patient states that he thinks that during the last week preceding the crime he had less pleasure in his anticipation"

He didn't take the same pleasure in thinking of getting ten thousand dollars by kidnaping, the last week, because the murder began to worry him, and he was going to make Leopold share the guilt equally of the murder This man who does not believe in God, and certainly does not believe in the laws of the State of Illinois, who has no emotions or heart, might be surprised to know that it was his own conscience bothering him the last week

"He did not want to back out, because of their

extensive plans, because of the time spent, because of the trouble they had gone to, and because of his associate being in it with him, and he was afraid of what the associate would think, should he not go ahead. They decided to get any young boy they knew to be of a wealthy family." Oh, no, money didn't enter into it.

Again, "They had also perfected the plan for securing"— what? The thrill? The excitement? "They had also perfected the plan for securing the money. The victim's father was to be told to put the money in a cigar box." I won't go on with that, because your Honor is familiar with the details.

Again on page 107, the doctors say, continuing with Loeb "We got the boy and disposed of him as planned on Wednesday. We returned the car to the agency at 4 30." And the doctors remark in parenthesis, "At this point he choked up and he wiped his nose with his fingers. He wiped away the tears." No emotion?

The other fellow hasn't any emotions either your Honor, none at all. He drove them all out when he was seven or eight or nine or ten years of age at the same time he passed God out of his heart. Well, let's see what Dickie says about it "I had quite a time quieting down my associate (after the murder) I cooled him down in five minutes, after we got him (Bobby Franks) into the back seat thinking he was alive. I got calmer while quieting my associate Franks was hit on the head several times My associate said, 'This is terrible, this is terrible.'"

I will tell your Honor, if you don't think they have emotions, of another instance. Some of us didn't think that Harvey Church had. He told his story with the air of braggadocio, and he gloated, apparently, while he was telling the authorities how tough a fellow he was. But when he was told to begin his march to the gallows, they carried him there in a stupor.

And if it is the fate of these two cowardly perverts that they must pay the penalty of this crime upon the gallows, when they realize it, you will find that they have emotions, and you will find they have fear, and you will find they will have to be carried to the gallows.

Cold-blooded? How did they put this poor little Franks boy into the culvert? There is that little dead body, naked, and after they shoved it in they kicked it in. And, according to Loeb, "Unfortunately the body was not kicked far enough into this hole, because a foot remained protruding, visible to a passer-by."

That was the only unfortunate thing about this, that a foot stuck out. The body was found the next day, and they are sitting before your Honor on a plea of guilty to this murder.

On page 110 "He first stated that he got more of a kick out of discussing it with his own family, but later changed his statement, and said that he felt he got a little less kick, because he had some slight remorse. His mother said that whoever did it should be tarred and feathered."

What does that mean? A mob ought to take him? We have heard Mr Darrow talk repeatedly of the hoarse cry of the angry mob. There is no danger or fear about hearing the hoarse cry of the angry mob, if the extreme penalty is visited here. I am not so sure, otherwise.

"On the other hand, the patient was a little worried"—well, what is worry? Worry is an emotion, the same as fear, the same as love. "Worried by the attitude of his father."

Now, let us find out how he has acted in jail. On page 114. "He has shown nothing unusual in his behavior in jail."

Of course, after this report had been given to the lawyers and the doctors from the East, they had to add to it a little bit, just as they did about the epilepsy, and Doc White brought in a lot of things that are not in this report, and some one else brought the unusual conduct of the defendant while he was in jail, wearing an old coat, and so on. But these two doctors, when the defense was young and had not matured, say he showed nothing unusual in his behavior in jail.

"His life is quiet and well ordered. Eats and sleeps well, even going to sleep while his associate was being examined in the same room."

The Loeb-Leopold Case

Dr Krohn has been criticized for saying that these defendants were correctly oriented in all three manners. Let us see what *their* doctors say "He is correctly oriented in the three spheres."

He knows his name, he knows where he is, he knows what is going on

"He takes a lively interest in the jail routine, and in the affairs of other prisoners, speaking of their crimes and their prospects in the usual jail phraseology, 'Such and so-and-so will get the rope,' or 'I think so-and-so will get the street.'"

Is there anything in his conduct in the jail that those doctors discovered to indicate a boy who wants to do a mad act? Or is it just the conduct of normal people, people who are responsible to the law for their violations of it?

Your Honor, I want to call your attention to one or two little things which show that this was not a purposeless crime of mad boys traveling around in a dream. On page 105 of the Hulbert-Bowman report, the doctors say "The boys arranged to have their rented car, with a black cloth over the license plate, backed up to the tracks, at the place where the box would be thrown. They had timed the train, they had arranged that if the train was late, it probably meant that there had been some flaws in their plans, and that the father had sought aid, whereupon they would drive away in the car and not wait for the train."

Planning, deliberating, working out the most

minute details, they were perfectly assured that their plans were so perfect that they themselves would never be suspected, and of course would never be apprehended

And nothing, in my judgment, but an act of God, an act of Providence, is responsible for the unraveling of this terrible crime I think that when the glasses that Leopold had not worn for three months, glasses that he no longer needed, dropped from his pocket at night, the hand of God was at work in this case He may not have believed in a God But if he has listened and paid attention and thought as the evidence was unfolded, he must begin to believe there is a God now

I have referred to the fact that they tried to create an impression that when the doctors were examining them they were perfectly frank, they cooperated, they did not lie, they did not distort, they did not hold back any evidence, and that is the sworn testimony of the three doctors from the East

Let us find out whether that is true or not I suspected and I tried to get them to admit on cross-examination that boys of superior education and intellect, boys who could plan a crime of this sort stretching over a period of six months and attend to every minute detail, boys who showed such an abandoned and malignant heart as the facts in this case show that they possessed, might possibly, when caught like rats, lie just a little bit to friendly doctors who were trying to build up a defense for them to save their worthless lives Oh, no, that is impossible. Everything they told us was true They withheld nothing. They distorted nothing They suppressed nothing.

Well, let's see what they say about it in the report that was intended to be a secret report and was not to fall into your hands or mine. On page 115, if your Honor please, in a friendly psychiatric examination " The boy is apparently frank, but is not absolutely so, sometimes distorting his statements, but without anything to indicate it, and sometimes suppresses much data."

I wonder whether it is possible they did fool Old Doc Yak from Washington, and I wonder whether it was necessary to fool him

Back to the motive again, on page 116 " He had no hatred toward the boy As the hate of his first planned victim disappeared, the excitement of planning grew, and money developed as an afterthought Neither he nor his associate would have done it without the money That extra $5,000 would have been his security" And then the doctor, quoting the language of Loeb in quotation marks, says· " And $5 000 is $5,000 "

Have they any interest in the money? On page 118, your Honor " We anticipated especially the money," in the language of Loeb, and then the doctor adds in parenthesis, " Facial expression of interest " " We thought we had it all so cleverly worked out, and we felt certain at not being caught, or we would not have gone into it "

Is that the mad talk of a mad man or a mad boy? Or is that the cold-blooded reasoning of a man who is a criminal, with a criminal heart and a superior intelligence and education?

" I had considered the possibility of being caught and I was afraid my father, a sick man, could not stand the shock, but I felt so certain of not being caught that we went on with it' No emotion Just a machine And yet again, on page 118, if your Honor please, the doctor says " He expressed remorse " At what? At his being caught The only one that he is concerned in, in his scheme of life, is himself

" I asked him if he would go through this plan again if he felt certain he would not be discovered He replied ' I believe I would, if I could get the money' The patient's attention was called to a newspaper account of an interview with Mrs Franks, the mother of the victim, in which she stated she had no desire to see the boys hanged, but would like to talk to them to know whether the boy suffered in his last moments The patient was asked whether it would upset him at all to talk with Mrs Franks He replied, he thought it would upset him a little, and make him feel sad He said when he read this interview in the paper, ' My first feeling was joy ' "

Joy at what? " ' That it might help us, her not

feeling vindictive Then a little remorse, not much, perhaps a little bit '"

His emotions respond not much when he thinks of the suffering of Mrs Franks, but when he thinks that her statement might save his neck, he experiences great joy No emotion?

Again, on page 119 " The patient stated that although he had no feeling of remorse about the crime, he felt very, very sorry about it for his family's sake, because it might cause them distress ' I would be willing to increase the chance of my hanging to save the family from believing that I was the archfiend My folks have probably had the blow softened by blaming him (Leopold) and his folks by blaming me, but before I decide to take the responsibility in order to save my family, I must consult with my elder brother '"

Everything he said and told the doctors, he told it on advice, and repeatedly this report demonstrates that

There has been some talk here, in order to make him appear to be mad, that he even contemplated killing his little brother Tommy, or killing his father The evidence in this case shows that that is just thrown in for good measure, that it has no foundation in fact at all It is another piece of perjury manufactured in order to build a foundation for a perjured insanity defense

On page 120, if your Honor please, when questioned about his attitude toward his family, the

The Loeb-Leopold Case

questioning was directed toward the possibility of some of them having been considered as the victim of this superior crime. It does not emanate from him, and it does not emanate from Leopold. The doctor suggested it to him. " The questioning was directed toward the possibility of some of them having been considered. He described having in a joking way proposed that his own younger brother Tommy be the victim, and his associate jokingly agreed with it, but they gave up the idea because it was not practical, for this reason that Tommy having disappeared, the patient would have to be at home, and with the family, during the period of the hunt, and could not be footloose to carry out the plans of securing the ransom money. 'I couldn't have done it, because I am tremendously fond of him.'"

Emotion, love. After this had been suggested to him, still they thought of money, money, money. If they kidnaped one of the fathers he asked who would furnish the money. They thought again that it was not practicable, that there would be no one to furnish the money.

Again, on page 121, if your Honor please. " He had proposed that with his associate, and with his associate had contemplated, using Dick Rubel, a very close friend of the patient and his associate, toward whom neither the patient nor his associate had any ill feeling or grudge as a victim." On page 122 " The plan of kidnaping Dick Rubel was given

The Loeb-Leopold Case

up, because Dick Rubel's father was so tight we might not get any money from him."

And, also, another reason — it runs all through. First, the necessity of getting the money, and, second, the necessity of avoiding detection. And on page 122: "And, furthermore, they might be suspected, because they were such close friends, and associated so much with him. Therefore, they would be sure to be questioned if Dick Rubel should disappear."

Now, I told your Honor about A, B, C and D, that these doctors decided that it was forensically inadvisable to go into, and for that reason they did not go into it. I told you at that time that I would prove by this report that Loeb had committed major crimes, four of them, that he would not even tell his lawyers about, that he would not tell the doctors about, and that they concluded it was a bad thing to make inquiry about, that Leopold knew about these, and that Loeb was afraid of Leopold, that he contemplated killing him so that he would not be in his power.

Now, let us see what the evidence is on that. "The patient and his associate were on very intimate terms, but the patient stated that his associate often stated that he would never entirely trust the patient, since the time the associate had found the patient was taking unfair financial advantage of him." Or, in other words, that he did not have the honor that is supposed to exist among thieves, Loeb was robbing Leopold. 'In a way, I have always been sort of afraid of him. He intimidated me by threatening to expose me, and I could not stand it." And on page 123: 'Of late the patient, Loeb, had often thought of the possibility of shooting his associate." He was afraid of Leopold, he was afraid that Leopold might tell of A, B, C and D.

And again, on page 123, your Honor: "He often contemplated shooting his associate when they were out together and they had the associate's revolvers along. He thought of pointing the revolver at his associate and shooting him. He denied ever having thought of hitting him over the head with a chisel. 'The idea of murdering a fellow, especially alone, I don't think I could have done it. If I could have snapped my fingers and made him pass away in a heart attack, I would have done it.'"

Now we can understand why the doctors in their testimony suppressed this part of the testimony. Now we can understand what A, B, C and D are. On page 124: "One reason why he never murdered" Leopold — the report says "associate" — "was that he felt that he would be suspected and there was no very safe way of doing it."

I have demonstrated by their own evidence, your Honor, that money was the underlying motive of the whole thing, and that they were not going to kill anybody if they thought there was a possibility of being caught. They did not kill the first man they had in mind because he was a larger man than they. Always that concern about their own precious hides.

And one reason why he did not kill Leopold was because he knew of no safe way of doing it and he might have been suspected. Well, it might have been a good thing if he could have planned a safe way to kill Leopold as he did to kill Bobby Franks and then have stopped there, or he might have carried it a little further and committed suicide. The community might have been grieved but I do not think it would have lasted long.

"In connection with this he had often contemplated murdering his associate and securing a new pal."

Somebody who would have nothing on him.

"He states that he had often contemplated hitting his associate over the head with a pistol, later shooting him, breaking the crystal of his watch, robbing him, leaving things in a way to create the effect that his associate had been robbed but there had been a struggle and he had been killed during the struggle."

Money, and his opinion of the power of money. He thought that on account of his millions or his father's millions he was above the law. He believed that you cannot hang a million dollars in Cook County no matter how dastardly the crime. Well, I disagree with him. I think the law is superior to money.

I direct your Honor's attention to page 126. "He

The Loeb-Leopold Case

contemplated escape from jail, but he does not want to do this for it would distress his family to have him disappear and to be known either as a criminal or an insane person. Before he decides to escape he wanted to discuss this with his older brother Allen. He thinks " — and this is his philosophy, and I don't know but what it was quite a coincidence that one of the books he took to the Morrison Hotel was the "Influence of Wealth on Imperial Rome," but it is his philosophy here, your Honor — " He thinks an escape could be managed by spending a few thousand dollars by bribing the guards of the jail and by some one giving him a gun. He says that, without any swagger, as though it were only a matter of careful detailed planning which his mind can do. He has not made plans as to where he should go should he escape." Then the doctors add "It must be borne in mind that Tommy O'Connor, one of the most desperate and one of the most intelligent criminals Chicago has ever known, did a most successful jail delivery from this jail within the last few years."

What a feeling of comfort and security mothers and fathers of this town would have, with their children going back and forth upon the streets of Chicago to school, and these two mad dogs at large.

Let us find out about this superman stuff. Page 127 "He often discussed morals with his associate, who insisted to him that the only wrong he, the patient, can do is to make a mistake, that anything that gives him pleasure is right for him to do "

Let's find out what judgment and credence Loeb pays to that statement He knew Leopold, and he knew when Leopold was joking and he knew when he was in earnest, and when he talked about the superman theory, he says "I took it with a great big dose of salt " But the doctors swallowed it as if it was sugar Any emotion? Page 128 " He says he is now sorry for his present predicament " It reminds me of a fellow who killed his wife some years ago and when his lawyer went in to talk to him he had no defense on earth At that time these nameless insanity diseases were not thought of and it looked as if this fellow was going to hang, and he afterwards did, and he told the lawyer with tears running down his cheeks, " You know there isn't anybody in town who feels as bad about this as I do "

There isn't anybody in town that feels as bad as Loeb does about his present predicament for his family's sake He says he should be sorrier He says it is wrong He doesn't know what should be done to him He felt that the law should take its course unless he could avoid it in some other way One hurdle at a time is his theory and Darrow's theory, to beat the rope Talk about life imprisonment in the penitentiary Escape if you can and if you cannot the same arguments that we made to save your necks we will make to the Board of Par-

The Loeb-Leopold Case

dons or the Governor and get you out. He would repeat maybe if he knew he would not be discovered. Is that mitigation, your Honor? All the way through this report runs the statement "I would kill again if I thought I would get away with it," and they offer that in mitigation for a murder.

"When he and his associate quarreled in March the patient considered securing another friend for his criminal operations. He actually hinted concerning this to his friend, but as he met with no favorable response he did not press the matter further. As he had considered that he and his associate would be no longer together after June of this year" (that is when Leopold would be in Europe) "he had thought of other ways of continuing his career of crime" (A, B, C, D, and the Franks murder is E!) "One idea was to rent a room in a bad neighborhood and hang around poolrooms and meet criminals. He had also considered becoming a clever financial criminal."

Money, money, money, not thrill, not excitement. A clever financial criminal, after he finished his law courses. He stated that he had considered crimes similar to that of Koretz, who had put through a gigantic stock swindle. If Mr. Darrow had read this, I think he would have blamed Koretz for this murder.

Heredity, finally Mr. Darrow says, the family, or some ancestor away back, planted the seed here. Hereditary influence. Well, let's see what their doctors say, on page 139 " There is nothing about the patient's condition to show any evidence of a hereditary nature, and there is not the slightest reason to suppose that a condition of this kind will be transmitted to future generations by any of his relatives This condition is acquired within the life history of the individual, and dies out when he dies There is nothing elicited from a most careful and painstaking history from all possible sources, to suggest that the family, either by omission or commission, contributed toward his delinquencies in the way they trained this boy "

Continuing with the Bowman-Hulbert report on page 100 — and here the person talking is Leopold, and not Loeb " The reason why they agreed to strangle the victim with a rope, to their mind, was that that would make them equally guilty of the crime It was not with any idea of close friendship or brotherhood, it was, rather, the opposite The patient did not like the idea of strangling the victim, and suggested chloroforming him, but his companion would not agree to this "

In other words, all this king-and-slave fantasy is a pure figment of the imagination of the defense The real tie that binds in this case is that one was a criminal and the other had something on him He was afraid of exposure, he contemplated murdering him, and the other one blackmailed him, in the manner that I have already indicated

Loeb wanted to shut the mouth of Leopold, and

then break with him. Leopold had enough on him, on A, B, C and D, and that is why he wanted Leopold to help him choke the life out of little Bobby Franks.

Again, on page 100 "Considerable trouble was experienced in perfecting a plan whereby they could secure" — what? The thrill? No — "the money, without exposing themselves to too much danger of being apprehended." And again, on page 100 "They wanted to divide the $10,000 ransom money equally."

No emotion in the superman Leopold? No he killed all his emotions before he came into court on the advice of counsel and the advice of doctors. But on page 102. "It was necessary to hit the victim several times over the head and he bled some. This upset the patient a great deal. He said to his companion, 'My God, this is awful.' He experienced a sinking feeling in the pit of his stomach. His hands trembled, he lost some of his self-control. His companion, however, laughed and joked and helped the patient to get back his self-control."

When they got to the culvert they found the boy had already died and they could not carry out their original scheme of strangling him with a rope. Again, on page 108 "Asked if he would commit another such a crime if he were certain that he could escape detection, he replied, 'I would not commit another such a crime because I realize that no one can ever be sure of escaping detection.'"

The Loeb-Leopold Case

On page 108, we learn that before he knew that he would have to chloroform his emotion and let intellect walk into the court alone, he stated that he is rather fond of small children, that he always wanted to take a crying child into his arms and comfort it On such occasions he almost noticed a functioning of his lachrymal glands

"While in the jail the patient has clearly been under considerable emotional tension, and is rather irritable at times"

"The patient ordinarily is able to make a calm and self-possessed appearance, and before reporters and visitors seems perfectly self-possessed and unconcerned On the other hand, when he does not feel the need for doing it, and when he is talking frankly with people and no longer posing, he shows a good deal of irritability and nervous tension"

When he is not posing to prepare a defense based on the fact that he has no emotion, these doctors say he shows a great deal of emotion He wouldn't lie either Why, your Honor, it really would be too bad if these two young fellows imposed on Old Doc Yak I showed to you what Loeb said he would do. I showed to you in this report what he has done He has lied repeatedly to the doctors He has lied under advice of counsel and family He has suppressed and distorted

Let's see what Leopold said he would do On page 109 "He seems to be reasonably frank during the examination, particularly with regard to his

The Loeb-Leopold Case

own feelings and emotions and his estimate of himself On the other hand, he undoubtedly omits certain data regarding some of his past experiences. He lied rather plausibly at times Later, when he realized that it was known that he was lying, he appeared perfectly unconcerned A number of times he inquired whether his story agreed with his companion's, and seemed to show a great deal of concern about this matter "

He wanted to know whether they had both learned their lesson in the same manner from their instructors and whether they were both telling the same story " In fact, he did this so crudely that it was apparent that he was concerned lest there be some failure of their stories to coincide "

In other words, both of them are lying, both of them have lied, both have suppressed things and hidden them from their doctors, and they had to do it in order to give a basis to that insanity defense here

Money! On page 111 " They also considered kidnaping their respective fathers, but this idea never got very far because the immediate objection of securing the money came to their minds"

Money is always uppermost in their minds when they talk about this kidnaping, and the murder, as I have explained, is an afterthought, in order to protect themselves Psychiatric observations! We live and learn

" Patient's (Leopold's) intellectual functions are

intact and he is quite obviously an individual of high intelligence He is correctly oriented, and in excellent contact with his surroundings'

The same argument was made by Mr Darrow with reference to Leopold as was made about Loeb First he began to blame the old German philosopher Nietzsche although every student in every university for the last 25 years has read his philosophy And then I guess he thought that would not do because if reading this philosophy would be an excuse for this crime, how about the countless thousands who have gone before and who are still reading this philosophy who lead decent, honorable lives? He did not have a poor old nurse in this case to blame, and he was not quite satisfied in blaming some remote ancestor, so he blames their parents, respectable, decent, law-abiding citizens The only unfortunate thing that ever came into their lives was to have a snake like Leopold in that decent family Casting blame where blame was not due, but where sympathy should go out as it does go out from the heart of every person in this community, to the respected families of these men

But Darrow says, ' No Save your sympathy for the boys Do not place the blame on the boys Place it on their families This is the result of heredity "

Well, let us see what the doctors say " However, it might be said that our present degree of knowledge gives us no reason to feel that a mental condition such as the patient's is of an hereditary nature, or that it will appear in future generations The family have apparently endeavored to do everything possible to bring the patient up in a suitable manner, and there has been no conscious error or neglect on their part "

Well, so much for the medical defense in this case

Your Honor, Mr Darrow has read to you poetry May I be permitted for a few moments to read you some prose?

The White House, Washington, D C , August 8, 1904

The application for commutation of sentence of John W Burley is denied This man committed the most heinous crime known to our laws Twice before he has committed crimes of a similar, but less terrible character In my judgment there is no reason whatever for paying heed to the allegations that he is not of sound mind, — allegations made after the trial and the conviction

Nobody would pretend that there has ever been any such degree of mental unsoundness shown as would make people even consider sending him to an asylum if he had not committed this crime Under such circumstances, he should certainly be esteemed sane enough to suffer the penalty for his monstrous deed I have scant sympathy with the plea of insanity advanced to save a man from the consequences of crime when unless that crime had been committed, it would have been impossible to persuade any reasonable authority to commit him to an asylum as insane Among the most dangerous criminals, and especially among those prone to commit this particular kind of offense, there are plenty of a temper so fiendish or brutal as to be incompatible with any other than a brutish order of intelligence, but these men are nevertheless responsible for their acts, and nothing more tends to encourage crime among such men than the belief that through the plea of insanity or any other method it is possible for them to escape paying the just penalty of their crimes The crime in question is one to the existence of which we largely owe the existence of that spirit of lawlessness which takes form in lynching It is a crime so revolting that the criminal is not entitled to one particle of sympathy from any human being It is essential that punishment for it should be not only as certain but as swift as possible The jury in this case did their duty by recommending the infliction of the death penalty It is to be regretted that we do not have special provision for more summary dealing with this type of cases

The more we do what in us lies to secure a certain and swift justice in dealing with these cases, the more effectively do we work against the growth of that lynching spirit which is so full of evil omen for these people, because it seeks to avenge one infamous crime by the commission of another of equal infamy The application is denied, and the sentence will be carried into effect

And in the case at bar your Honor no one ever suspected that these defendants were mentally diseased until after lawyers were retained to defend them and when there was no escape on the facts

If I had taken them into custody on the twentieth of May and had attempted to have them committed to an insane asylum, their lawyers, their doctors and their families would have been here and there would

The Loeb-Leopold Case

have been only one crazy man in the court room, namely, the State's Attorney

I submit, if your Honor please, that it is safer to follow the philosophy of Theodore Roosevelt as he laid it down in this great State paper, when he was President of the United States, and was only concerned with the enforcement of the law, than it is to follow the weird and uncanny philosophy of the paid advocate of the defense, whose business it is to make murder safe in Cook County

Now, if your Honor please, Mr Darrow argued that the State had advanced the silly argument that these boys were gamblers, and they gambled for high stakes, and he said the only evidence we had to predicate such a charge on was the testimony of Leon Mandel, who had played one game of bridge with them and who said that in that game they played for five or ten cents a point The trouble with Mr Darrow is that he does not know all the facts in this case, he does not know all the evidence

I thank God that I am not a great pleader, because I think sometimes when men are obsessed with the idea that when they open their mouths words of wisdom rush out, and that all that is necessary in the trial of a case is to make a wonderful argument, a great many of them fail, in my judgment, for those reasons, because they rely too much upon their oratory, they pay little attention to the facts in the case, and, after all, I believe that courts and juries are influenced, not by oratory but by hard facts sworn to by witnesses. That is why I have paid more attention to the preparation of the evidence in this case than I have to writing a closing speech.

Now, let us see if there is any other evidence in this case. Among the letters introduced in evidence we find one from Allen M. Loeb. Allen Loeb is the generalissimo of the defense; he is the one who is advising young Loeb whether or not he ought to tell the doctors this or whether he ought to tell the lawyers that. This letter was mailed May 19th at 5.30 P.M., 1924, and probably was received by Richard Loeb the day of the murder; marked "Personal."

Dear Dick: I wanted to send this letter to you so there would be no possible chance of Dad seeing it. Glad to hear about Sammy Schmaltz, but could that amount have been possibly reversed? If so, you are all wrong in your gambling, and even so, you must be shooting a little too high. Did you get cash, or did he pay on an I O U, I suppose? Best love,

ALLEN

"Could that amount have been possibly reversed?" Did you really win or did he?

Another letter from one of his companions, and it is fair to assume that he is a wealthy man, or the son of a wealthy man. It is written on the stationery of Robert L. Leopold, 530 Thompson Street, Ann Arbor, Michigan, and is as follows:

The Loeb-Leopold Case

Dear Dick Just a line, as I am awfully busy, and I am coming to you for help I have an exam in history, 17, and know nothing about it Furthermore, my notes are no good You said last semester that you would let me take your notes in the course Please send them to me right away if you can My exam is next Friday and I must study Please drop me a line and let me know, so I may know whether to plan on them or not I am damn sorry that we couldn t see each other while I was home, but you are always so ——— busy I guess I am, too, while home But I always feel as though I am intruding when you guys are gambling because I don't gamble that high At any rate better luck next time when home

                Thanks in advance for your trouble,

                              Sincerely,

                                    BOBBY

It is in evidence in this case, if your Honor please, that both of these defendants had a bank account We put a witness on the stand, an employe of Sears, Roebuck, who testified that from time to time she gave checks to the defendant Loeb here She told me about two checks for two hundred and fifty dollars, I am not quite certain about the date and I want to be accurate

His allowance was $250 a month, so they say The Charlevoix Bank statement shows that he deposited on March 15, 1923, $141 55, March 25, $125 00, May 16, $345 00, May 31, $300 00 All this was in 1923 June 28 $683 00, July, $171 40, July 13, $259 00, July 16, $108 00, July 21, $50.00,

The Loeb-Leopold Case

August 27, $155 00, August 28, $175 00, September 8, $300 00, September 19, $302 75

Where did he get it? These are not checks for $250 00 from Sears, Roebuck

Then he had another account at the Hyde Park State Bank It shows as follows on deposits October 1, 1923, $485 00, October 16, $50 00, November 1, $444 50, November 5, $100 00, November 16, $100 00, November 19, $730 00, November 28, $175 00

Business was good that month. December 24, $400 00, February 6, $425 00

That is this year February 14, $230 00, March 14, $137 00, April 16 $350 00; April 25, $100 00, May 15, $536 51 This was the week before the murder and where did he get it? April 16, $350 00, April 25, $100 00 That is 1924 Where did he get it?

Mr Darrow Do you know whether any of those checks were from one bank to the other?

Mr Crowe I don't know, Mr Darrow

Mr Darrow It might be well to look into it.

Mr Crowe He didn't get it from his father in those amounts and at those times Would A, B, C and D explain it or was it won in gambling?

There has been testimony here that he had Liberty bonds, and had not clipped the coupons from them for two or three years Well, if they were the proceeds of a robbery, that was an act of wisdom and discretion

Now, if your Honor please, in support of our contention that the motive in this case was, first, money, that the original crime planned was the crime of kidnaping, that murder was later decided upon in order to protect them from arrests and punishment, I do not intend to take up your Honor's time by reviewing all the evidence independently of the statements made by these defendants to their doctors that I have read to you from the Bowman-Hulbert report but I will direct your Honor's attention to the " uncomfortable afternoons " that they spent along the Illinois Central tracks, the number of times they threw a pad of paper from the car to see where the money would light I will direct your attention again to the ransom letter " Secure before noon today $10,000 This money must be composed entirely of old bills '

If they merely wanted to get the money and did not want to use it, what difference whether the bills were old, what difference whether they were marked or unmarked if they did not intend to spend them?

As a final word of warning " This is a strictly commercial proposition " All the way through, if your Honor please, all the way through this most unusual crime runs money, money, money And when it is not money it is blood I think that we have clearly established the real motive in this case

Mr Darrow relies upon the facts, first, he says there was no motive, second, upon the youth of the defendants, and, third, upon their mental condition

The Loeb-Leopold Case

I think I have demonstrated beyond doubt that the controlling motive in this case was money, $10,000 and as much more as they could get afterwards

Now, how about their health? Leopold has a calcified pineal gland Dr Woodyatt said that did not mean anything Nobody knows, and nobody has testified on behalf of the defense that it did mean anything Glands, they tell us, do not generally calcify until you are about thirty years of age Now, some people develop earlier in life than others I believe, in Africa, women are matured at nine years of age and bear children at nine or ten years of age Leopold has developed a little earlier than the average man He has developed sexually and mentally and if it means anything at all it means that he has the intellect and brain and mind of a man thirty years of age and that is all

Doctors Hulbert and Bowman said there was not anything pathological about Loeb except the minus 17 on his basal metabolism And every doctor who took the stand said that that was within the range of normality

Why, your Honor can look at them You have looked at them You have observed them There is nothing the matter with them physically There is nothing the matter with them mentally The only fault is the trouble with their moral sense, and that is not a defense in a criminal case

Your Honor, Conners, 22 years of age, a Cairo

negro, was sentenced July 31 for a crime of murder on a plea of guilty

I submit, if we can take the flower of American manhood, take the boys at 18 years of age and send them to their death in the front line trenches of France in defense of our laws, we have an equal right to take men 19 years of age and take their lives for violating those laws that these boys gave up their lives to defend Ah, many a boy 18 years of age lies beneath the poppies in Flanders fields who died to defend the laws of this country

We might direct your Honor's attention to what is going on over this land right at this time while this case is on trial Alexander Bujec, 19, must die in the electric chair October 17, for the murder of his 13-year-old cousin in Akron, Ohio. He was sentenced August 20

Mr Darrow has referred in the case to hanging Mr Darrow is a student of criminology, he has written a book on it and he says the criminal age, the time when crimes are committed, is between the ages of 17 and 24 And your Honor and I know that the average criminal age is 22 If we are going to punish crime and by the punishment stop it, and the criminal age is between 17 and 24, how can we punish it if the age is a defense?

Mr Darrow criticised Mr Marshall for his quotations from Blackstone, and seemed to be under the impression that we were trying to try this case under the ancient British law We are trying this case, if your Honor please, under the statutes of the State of Illinois in the year 1924. The statute that your Honor is bound to enforce in this case, and the statute under which we are trying these defendants, provides that from 14 years of age up the law presumes that one has the capacity to commit a crime and is entirely responsible for it

Let us see at what age some of these men have been hanged Buff Higgins was hanged at the age of 23 Butch Lyons was 25 Henry Foster, 24 Albert C Fields, 24 Windreth, 29 Mannow, 27. Dan McCarty, 27 William T Powers, 23 Chris Murray, 28 John Drugan, 22 Robert Howard, 30 Louis Pesant, sentenced on a plea of guilty April 15, 1904, by Judge Kernsten, was 23 Peter Neidermeyer, 23 Gustave Marks, 21 Harvey Van Dine, 21

These were not the poor sons of multimillionaires, these were the sons of poor men, who had no advantages in life, men who had no education, men who had been brought up in the gutter and the slums

Richard Ivens, 24 Andrew Williams, 22 Thomas Jennings, 28 Thomas Schultz, 19 Frank Shiblewski, 22, and his brother hanged the same day. Ewald, 23. Smith, 27 Lundgren, 25 Dennis Anderson, 21. Lloyd Bopp, 23. Albert Johnson, 25 Earl Dear, 26 Jack O'Brien, 22 Mills, 21. Champion, 22 Zander, 22

Haensel, a man who fought for his country, who

was syphilitic, who was hit in the service of his country in the head by a chain weighing a thousand pounds, and who was discharged from further service physically unfit, was hanged in Cook County at the age of 27. The little songbird from Italy, Viani, 17. Brislane, 27. Sam Ferrari, 26. Oscar McDavit, a colored man who thought that the Lord had appointed him to lead his race back to Africa, 23. George Brown, 29. Antonio Lopez, 26. Harry Ward, 25. Carl Wanderer, 25. Ligregni, 27. Harvey Church, 23. Pastoni, 26.

Dalton, sentenced by your Honor, a colored boy, without any of the advantages that these men had, whose ancestors were slaves, only two or three generations removed from savagery in Africa, and yet he paid the penalty for the violation of the laws.

Walter Krauser, sitting in the county jail, marking off the days between now and the day he hangs, 21. Bernard Grant, sitting in the county jail, waiting for October 17, when he will pay the penalty upon the gallows.

Oh, but Mr. Darrow says there are only four men who have been hanged on pleas in Cook County.

Now, your Honor and I are familiar enough with the practice over here not to be fooled by that. What happens when a man gets a guilty client and there is no defense? He generally goes to the State's Attorney, and he says, "If you will waive the death penalty I will plead guilty." If there are in the nature of the case any mitigating circumstances the State's Attorney says "Yes, we will waive the death penalty Let's go upstairs and plead him guilty, and I will recommend life"

But if the case is of such a nature that the State's Attorney cannot in conscience and in law waive the extreme penalty, he says "No, that man has got to go to a jury"

The reason that courts do not hang any oftener than they do is because hanging cases always go to juries Where the attorney cannot make an agreement in advance, he says. "Well, then, I am going to take a chance with 12 men They can't do any worse than the court can do on a plea, and I am going to give my client a run for his money"

Now, your Honor and I know that that is the case, and Mr Darrow knows it is the case, and everybody who is familiar with procedure in the Criminal Court knows it is the case. It is not because there is one law for the judge and another law for the jury It is not because juries must execute the law to the uppermost, and the court has a right to sit as a friendly father

That being the situation, are we going to tell the criminal world, and Mr Darrow says the criminal world is between 17 and 24, and the average is 22, the age at which murders are committed, crimes of violence are committed, are we going to tell them that the new law introduced into the statutes of Illinois by Clarence Darrow and approved by the

Chief Justice of the Criminal Court makes it perfectly safe for them to murder, or are we going to tell them that the law will be vigorously enforced? The law, if your Honor please, is made to protect the innocent, and it is made to protect the innocent by punishing the guilty and in no other way can we protect the innocent or protect society

I think, if your Honor please, I have now covered the three defenses set forth by Mr Darrow, their age, lack of motive, and physical and mental condition

When we get all through, Mr Darrow says that your Honor ought to be merciful and, finally, and that is his concluding defense, he appeals to your heart and your sympathy and not to your mind or your conscience

When I was listening to Mr Darrow plead for sympathy for these two men who showed no sympathy, it reminded me of a story of Abraham Lincoln's about a young boy about their age whose parents were wealthy and he murdered both of them. He was an only child and he did it so that he might inherit their money His crime was discovered the same as this crime has been discovered, and the court asked him for any reason he might have why sentence of death should not be passed upon him and he promptly replied that he hoped the court would be lenient to a poor orphan Robert Franks had a right to live He had a right to the society of his family and his friends and they had a right to his society. These two young law students of superior intelligence, with more intelligence than they have heart, decided that he must die. He was only 14. These two law students knew under the law if you had a right to take a life you had a right to take it at 14, and they thought they had a right to take his life, and they proceeded to take it.

Mr. Darrow quoted considerable poetry to you, and I would like again to be indulged while I read a little prose. This is from an address delivered by Clarence Darrow to the prisoners in the county jail, if your Honor please.

Crime and Criminals. If I looked at jails and crime and prisoners in the way the ordinary person does, I should not speak on this subject to you. The reason I talk to you on the question of crime, its cause and cure, is because I really do not believe in the least in crime. There is no such thing as a crime, as the word is generally understood. I do not believe that there is any sort of distinction between the real moral condition in and out of jail. One is just as good as the other. The people here can no more help being here than the people outside can avoid being outside. I do not believe people are in jail because they deserve to be. They are in jail simply because they cannot avoid it, on account of circumstances which are entirely beyond their control, and for which they are in no way responsible. I suppose a great many people on the outside would say I was doing you harm, if they should hear what I have to say to you this afternoon, but you cannot be hurt a great deal, anyway, so it will not matter. The good people outside would say that I was really teaching you things that are calculated to injure society, but it is worth while, now

The Loeb-Leopold Case

and then to hear something different from what you ordinarily get from preachers and the like. They will tell you that you should be good, and then you will be rich and happy. Of course, we know that people don't get rich by being good, and that is the reason why so many of you people try to get rich some other way; only you don't understand how to do it quite as well as the fellow outside.

There are people who think that everything in this world is an accident, but really there is no such thing as an accident. A great many persons feel that many of the people in jail ought to be there, and many of those outside ought to be in. I think none of them ought to be here. There ought to be no jails, and if it were not for the fact that the people on the outside are so grasping and heartless in their dealing with the people on the inside, there would be no such institutions as jails.

When I ride on the street cars I am held up, I pay five cents a ride for what is worth two and a half cents, simply because a body of men have bribed the City Council and the Legislature so that all the rest of us have to pay tribute to them. If I don't want to fall into the clutches of the gas trust, and choose to burn oil instead of gas, then good Mr Rockefeller holds me up.

Let me see whether there is any connection between the crime of the respectable classes and your presence in the jail. Many of you I believe are in jail because you have really committed burglary, many of you because you have stolen something within the meaning of the law, you have taken some other person's property. Some of you may have entered a store and carried off a pair of shoes because you did not have the price. Possibly some of you have committed murder. I cannot tell what all of you did. There are a great many people here who have done some of these things, who really don't know themselves why they did them. I think I know why you did them, every one of you. You did these things because you were bound to do them. It looked to you at the time as if you had a chance to do them or not, as you saw fit, but still, after all, you had no choice. There are many people who had some money in their pocket and still went out and got some more money in a way society forbids.

Now, you may not yourself see exactly why it was you did this, but if you look at the question deeply enough and carefully enough you will see that there were circumstances that drove you to do exactly the thing which you did. You could not help it, any more than we outside can help taking the position we will take. The reformers will tell you to be good and you will be happy, and people who have property to protect think the only way to do is to build jails and lock you up on week days and pray for you on Sundays.

I think all this has nothing whatever to do with right conduct. Some so-called criminals — and I will use that word, because it is handy, it means nothing to me, I speak of the criminal who gets caught as distinguished from the criminal who catches them — some of these so-called criminals are in jail for the first offense, but nine-tenths of you are in jail because you did not have a good lawyer, and of course you did not have a good lawyer because you did not have enough money to pay a good lawyer. There is no very great danger of a rich man going to jail.

There is a bill before the Legislature of this State, to punish the kidnaping of children with death. We have wise members of the Legislature. They know the gas trust when they see it — and they always see it. It can furnish light enough to be seen. And this Legislature thinks it is going to stop kidnaping of children, by making a law punishing kidnapers of children to death

I believe that progress is purely a question of the pleasurable units that we get out of life The pleasure-and-pain theory is the only correct theory of morality, and the only way of judging life

That is the doctrine of Leopold That is the doctrine expounded last Sunday in the press of Chicago by Clarence Darrow

I want to tell you the real defense in this case, your Honor, it is Clarence Darrow's dangerous philosophy of life He said to your Honor that he was not pleading alone for these two young men He said he was looking to the future, that he was thinking of the ten thousand young boys who in the future would fill the chairs his clients filled, and he wants to soften the law He wants them treated, not with the severity that the law of his State prescribes, but with kindness and consideration

I want to tell your Honor that it would be much better if God had not caused this crime to be disclosed, it would be much better if it had gone unsolved, and these men went unwhipped of justice, it would not have done near the harm to this community that will be done if your Honor, as Chief Justice of this great court, puts your official seal of approval upon the doctrines of anarchy preached by Clarence Darrow as a defense in this case Society can endure, the law can endure, if criminals escape, but if a court such as this court should say that he believes in the doctrines of Darrow, that you ought not to hang when the law says you should, a greater blow has been struck to our institutions than by a hundred, aye, a thousand murders

There is another matter, your Honor, to which Mr Darrow referred. Now, I do not want to refer to this any more than Mr Darrow did, but he referred to it and it is in evidence. Mr Darrow asked your Honor to believe that Gortland lied in his testimony about a "friendly judge."

On June 10, 1924, in the Chicago *Herald* and *Examiner* — that was before this case had been assigned to anybody, that was when Darrow was announcing, and he did announce in this same article, that they were going to plead not guilty — there was an article written by Mr Slattery, sitting back there, in which it was said "The friendly-judge resort suggested for the defense will be of no avail It was mentioned as a possibility that a plea of guilty might be entered, on the understanding it would result in life sentences If this becomes an absolute probability, Crowe announced that he will nolle prosse the case and re-indict the slayers"

Did Gortland lie? He gave the name of witness after witness that he told the story to, as he told it to Slattery, before the case was even assigned He says that was told to him by Leopold I don't know whether your Honor believes that officer or not; but I want to tell you, if you have observed these two defendants during the trial, if you have observed the conduct of their attorneys and their families — with one honorable exception, and that is the old man who sits in sackcloth and ashes, and who is entitled to the sympathy of everybody, old Mr Leopold — with that one honorable exception, everybody connected with the case has laughed and sneered and jeered, and if the defendant Leopold did not say that he would plead guilty before a friendly judge, his actions demonstrate that he thinks he has got one

You have, your Honor, listened with a great deal of patience and kindness and consideration to the State and the defense I am not going to trespass unduly upon your Honor's time, and I am going to close for the State I believe that the facts and circumstances proved in this case demonstrate that a crime has been committed by these two defendants, and that no other punishment than the extreme penalty of the law will fit it; and I leave the case with you on behalf of the State of Illinois, and I ask your Honor in the language of Holy Writ to " Execute justice and righteousness in the land."

Judge Caverly took exception to the remarks of Mr Crowe relative to the "friendly judge" suggestion, "as being a cowardly and dastardly assault upon the integrity of this court"

Mr Crowe It was not so intended, your Honor——

The Court And it could not have been used for any other purpose except to incite the mob and to try and intimidate this court It will be stricken from the record

Mr Crowe If your Honor please, the State's Attorney had no such intention——

The Loeb-Leopold Case

The Court We will go on ——

Mr Crowe I merely want to put my personal feelings plainly before the court It was not the intention of the State's Attorney ——

The Court The State s Attorney knew that would be heralded all through this country and all over this world, and he knows the court hadn't an opportunity except to do what he did It was not the proper thing to say This court will not be intimidated by anybody at any time or place so long as he occupies this position

The court then took the case under advisement, remarking that it had been a record one for speed, due to the "able manner in which the State s Attorney investigated and prepared his case for trial"

On Sept 10 the decision was announced both defendants being sentenced to the penitentiary for life

In connection with the formal sentences the court rendered the following opinion

In view of the profound and unusual interest that this case has aroused not only in this community but in the entire country and even beyond its boundaries, the court feels it his duty to state the reasons which have led him to the determination he has reached

It is not an uncommon thing that pleas of guilty are entered in criminal cases, but almost without exception in the past such pleas have been the result of a virtual agreement between the defendant and the State's Attorney whereby in consideration of the plea, the State's Attorney consents to recommend to the court a sentence deemed appropriate by him, and, in the absence of special reasons to the contrary it is the practice of the court to follow such recommendations

In the present case the situation is a different one A plea of guilty has been entered by the defense without a previous understanding with the prosecution and without any knowledge whatever on its part Moreover, the plea of guilty did not in this particular case, as it usually does, render the task of the prosecution easier by substituting admission of guilt for a possibly difficult and uncertain chain of proof

Here the State was in possession not only of the essential, substantiating facts but also of voluntary confessions on the part of the defendants. The plea of guilty, therefore, does not make a special case in favor of the defendants.

Since both of the cases, that, namely of murder and that of kidnaping for ransom, were of a character which invested the court with discretion as to the extent of the punishment, it became his duty under the statute to examine witnesses as to the aggravation and mitigation of the offense. This duty has been fully met. By consent of counsel for the State and for the defendants, the testimony in the murder case has been accepted as equally applicable to the case of kidnaping for ransom. In addition, a prima facie case was made out for the kidnaping case as well.

The testimony introduced both by the prosecution and the defense, has been as detailed and elaborate as though the case had been tried before a jury. It has been given the widest publicity, and the public is so fully familiar with all its phases that it would serve no useful purpose to restate or analyze the evidence.

By pleading guilty, the defendants have admitted legal responsibility for their acts, the testimony has satisfied the court that the case is not one in which it would have been possible to set up successfully the defense of insanity as insanity is defined and understood by the established law of this State for the purpose of the administration of criminal justice.

The court, however, feels impelled to dwell briefly on the mass of data produced as to the physical mental and moral condition of the two defendants. They have been shown in essential respects to be abnormal, had they been normal they would not have committed the crime. It is beyond the province of this court, as it is beyond the capacity of human science in its present state of development, to predicate ultimate responsibility for human acts.

At the same time, the court is willing to recognize that the careful analysis made of the life history of the defendants and of their present mental, emotional and ethical condition has been of extreme interest and is a valuable contribution

The Loeb-Leopold Case

to criminology. And yet the court feels strongly that similar analyses made of other persons accused of crime would probably reveal similar or different abnormalities. The value of such tests seems to lie in their applicability to crime and criminals in general. Since they concern the broad questions of human responsibility and legal punishment, and are in no wise peculiar to these individual defendants, they may be deserving of legislative but not of judicial consideration. For this reason the court is satisfied that his judgment in the present case cannot be affected thereby.

The testimony in this case reveals a crime of singular atrocity. It is, in a sense, inexplicable, but it is not thereby rendered less inhuman or repulsive. It was deliberately planned and prepared for during a considerable period of time. It was executed with every feature of callousness and cruelty.

And here the court will say, not for the purpose of extenuating guilt, but merely with the object of dispelling a misapprehension that appears to have found lodgment in the public mind, that he is convinced by conclusive evidence that there was no abuse offered to the body of the victim. But it did not need that element to make the crime abhorrent to every instinct of humanity, and the court is satisfied that neither in the act itself nor in its motive or lack of motive, nor in the antecedents of the offenders, can he find any mitigating circumstances.

For both the crime of murder and kidnaping for ransom, the law prescribes different punishments in the alternative.

For the crime of murder the statute declares:

" Whoever is guilty of murder shall suffer the punishment of death, or imprisonment in the penitentiary for his natural life, or for a term not less than fourteen years. If the accused is found guilty by a jury, they shall fix the punishment by their verdict; upon a plea of guilty, the punishment shall be fixed by the court."

For the crime of kidnaping for ransom, the statute reads:

" Whoever is guilty of kidnaping for ransom shall suffer death, or be punished by imprisonment in the penitentiary for life, or any term not less than five years."

The Loeb-Leopold Case

Under the plea of guilty, the duty of determining the punishment devolves upon the court and the law indicates no rule or policy for the guidance of his discretion. In reaching his decision the court would have welcomed the counsel and support of others. In some States the legislature in its wisdom has provided for a bench of three judges to determine the penalty in cases such as this. Nevertheless, the court is willing to meet his responsibilities. It would have been the path of least resistance to impose the extreme penalty of the law. In choosing imprisonment instead of death the court is moved chiefly by the consideration of the age of the defendants boys of 18 and 19 years. It is not for the court to say that he will not in any case enforce capital punishment as an alternative, but the court believes that it is within his province to decline to impose the sentence of death on persons who are not of full age

This determination appears to be in accordance with the progress of criminal law all over the world and with the dictates of enlightened humanity. More than that, it seems to be in accordance with the precedents hitherto observed in this State. The records of Illinois show only two cases of minors who were put to death by legal process — to which number the court does not feel inclined to make an addition

Life imprisonment may not, at the moment, strike the public imagination as forcibly as would death by hanging, but to the offenders particularly of the type they are, the prolonged suffering of years of confinement may well be the severer form of retribution and expiation

The court feels it proper to add a final word concerning the effect of the parole law upon the punishment of these defendants. In the case of such atrocious crimes it is entirely within the discretion of the department of public welfare never to admit these defendants to parole. To such a policy the court urges them strictly to adhere. If this course is persevered in the punishment of these defendants will both satisfy the ends of justice and safeguard the interests of society

www.ingramcontent.com/pod-product-compliance
Lightning Source LLC
Chambersburg PA
CBHW080839160125
20473CB00012BA/690